Marble head thought to belong to King Attalos I (241–197 BC). Antikensammlung, Berlin

pergamum

Fatih Cimok

A T U R İ Z M Y A Y I N L A R I

Front cover
**Marble relief of the giant Alkyoneus from the eastern frieze of the altar of Zeus.
First half of the second century BC. Pergamum Museum, Berlin**

Back cover
Hellenistic fortifications of Pergamum. First half of the second century BC

Photographs
Cüneyt Baykurt

Graphic Design
Güzin Sancaklı

Filmset
Ram

Typesetting
A Turizm Yayınları

Printed at
Promat

First printing December 1993
Second printing July 1995

Publishers
A Turizm Yayınları Ltd. Şti.
Şifa Hamamı Sokak 18, Sultanahmet 34400, Istanbul
Tel: 0 (212) 517 44 72 - 517 44 74 - 516 24 97; Fax: 516 41 65

CONTENTS
INTRODUCTION
SIGHTSEEING IN PERGAMUM
UPPER ACROPOLIS (CITADEL)
MIDDLE ACROPOLIS
LOWER ACROPOLIS
TEMPLE OF SERAPIS (RED HALL)
HISTORY OF PERGAMUM

Opposite Marble relief from the northern frieze of the altar of Zeus. First half of the second century BC. Pergamum Museum, Berlin. It shows one of the pair of goddesses who overhelm two giants. They are thought to be the Moirae, the goddesses who decide the destiny of man. The one in the picture is seen pulling the Giant by his hair. Her other weapon-bearing hand is raised to give the latter the final blow. The Giant has raised one arm and with this hand he tries to rescue his hair from the clutch of the goddess. His other hand is also raised and pulling the elbow of the goddess.

Upper acropolis

Middle acropolis

Lower acropolis

Plan of acropolis

INTRODUCTION

Pergamum is one of the few ancient sites in the world that has preserved its original Hellenistic ruins and character to a very large extent. The objective of this book is to acquaint visitors with these ruins and help them to understand the history of Pergamum better.

In this volume the surviving ruins from the Hellenistic and Roman history of Pergamum are introduced one by one in the order of the sightseeing itinerary of the present day. These ruins begin with the heroon (a shrine dedicated to a deified or semideified dead person) situated in front of the gate of the upper acropolis (citadel) and terminate with the lower agora in the acropolis. An effort has been made to make these ruins more meaningful by including the art objects discovered during excavations and moved to museums in Bergama, Istanbul, Berlin or Paris, by including their pictures in the related chapters.

Most of the visitors to the acropolis of Pergamum unfortunately do not spare time for the middle and lower acropolis and are content with visiting just the upper acropolis (citadel). However, the days when visitors will leave their cars at the present day parking area and descend towards the skirt of the acropolis walking on the ancient main street and visiting all of the surviving ruins in the upper, middle and lower acropolis should not be very far off.

Throughout the text, while all the dates before Christ are referred to as BC, using AD for the dates after Christ has not been felt necessary. Also, most of the archaeological terms are explained in parantheses at appropriate places, often when they are used for the first time.

Fatih Cimok

7

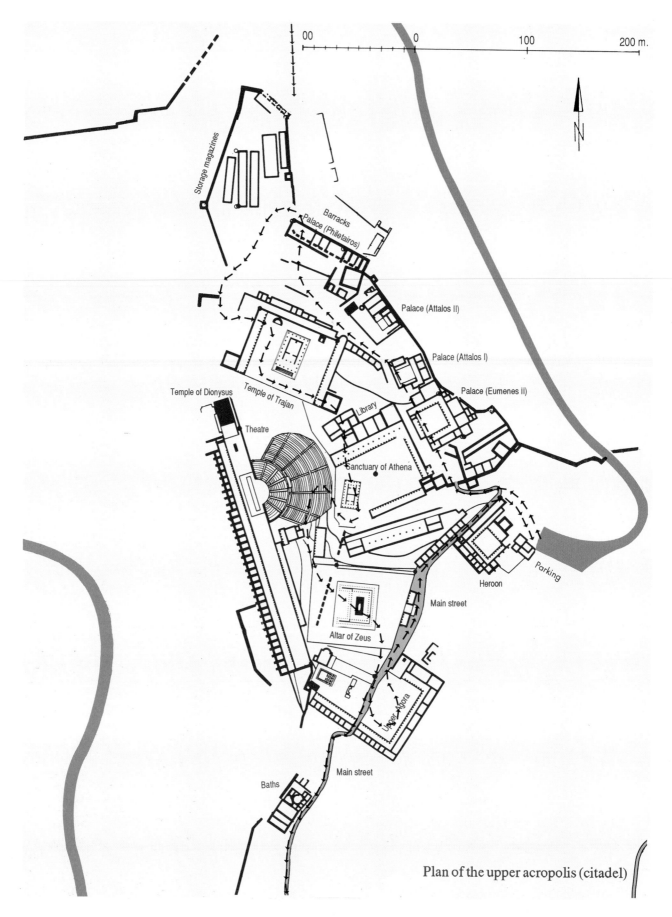

Plan of the upper acropolis (citadel)

8

SIGHTSEEING IN PERGAMUM

UPPER ACROPOLIS (CITADEL)

Almost all the ruins on the present day acropolis date from the Hellenistic era, when the kingdom of Pergamum was at the height of its power, and the city was a flourishing Hellenistic metropolis. The buildings to which these ruins belonged were built of gray-blue andesite, the original stone of the mountain which made excellent building material. The Roman additions, new monuments or reconstructions, were often in marble. However, since most of these marble constructions ended up in lime kilns during the centuries when such 'stones' were not important for people, or were moved to museums in the later period, what is left to the present day visitor is a genuine Hellenistic Pergamene acropolis, stripped of its Roman costume.

HEROON

The first group of surviving ruins on the acropolis is situated opposite the present day entrance, which was incidentally the original entrance of the citadel, dating back probably to the time before Philetarios, the actual founder of the kingdom of Pergamum. These ruins belong to a heroon where the cult of the Pergamene kings was celebrated. Ruler worship was one of the most characteristic phenomena of the Hellenistic period and was practised in Pergamum as well. However, unlike some other Hellenistic dynasties, the Attalid rulers were not recognized as gods in their lifetime but only honoured by special priesthood. They were deified, or 'translated to the gods' after death. Like the other Hellenistic rulers they bore titles such as Soter (Saviour), Epiphanes

Heroon

(God Manifest), or Euergetes (Benefactor).

The heroon of Pergamum consisted of a courtyard surrounded with columns on all sides (peristyle), an antechamber and a square cult room. The last two rooms stood on the north-eastern side. The antechamber is thought to have been used for the cult meals taken in honour of the deified Pergamene kings. Access to the building was gained by two doors from the main street which passed by the west side, and these were followed by long corridors. This Hellenistic building was mostly built of andesite and saw little alteration during the Roman period. In the excavations the ruins of some Hellenistic houses which stood here until the heroon was built were uncovered. The one referred to as the 'cistern-house' by archaeologists contains various sorts of channels and holes connected with water distribution. It is thought that this particular building was important enough for the water system of the city to be placed under the responsibility of an official, a sort of 'controller of the water supply'.

To the northwest of the heroon, the ruins of a row of twelve storage rooms from the Hellenistic period have been discovered.

After entering the citadel by the gate, which was flanked by guards' quarters, the paved street and the stairs lead directly to the palaces of the kings of Pergamum. On the left of the beginning of the road once stood the monumental entrance (propylon) of the sanctuary of Athena. When Philetairos was appointed as the governor of Pergamum, this hill, on which the most important edifices would later be built, was already a fortified citadel. The walls which surrounded it during this early period are thought to have been built in the fifth–fourth centuries BC. During the time of Philetairos the wall was enlarged in the southern direction as far as the sanctuary of Demeter, which it did not enclose.

Opposite, above Heroon. Detail from the west wall
Opposite, below Citadel

Heroon

PALACES

The palaces where the kings of Pergamum lived occupied the easternmost part of the citadel. The four building complexes, which had similar plans, that is a columned courtyard surrounded with various rooms (bedrooms, dining rooms, sitting rooms, kitchens, toilets, and suchlike), are tentatively ascribed to — from south to north — Attalos II, Eumenes II, Attalos I and Philetairos. However, when compared to the proverbial wealth of the kingdom they look like the remains of small and unpretentious structures. The western extensions of the palaces must have been levelled out in the Roman period to create room for the temple of Trajan.

The first two palaces are known as being among the earliest examples of the true peristyle plan. Some pieces stones which have been revealed in the first and the largest of these palace ruins, and which are thought to be shaped for the altar of Zeus, have led archaeologists to think that this building must have been the palace of Eumenes II during whose reign the altar was known to have been built. The research has

Palaces

Palaces. Cistern

Palaces. Overflow tank

shown that during the reign of this king marble was used in Pergamum together with the local stone of the mountain. The Roman period remains of the Hellenistic cistern which supplied water to this palace have survived on the right (eastern) side of the street.

There is not much left from the other palace buildings. The deep cylindrical cistern encountered in this area is thought to be related to the central water tower which must have been built on the highest spot of the acropolis. At present this spot is occupied by a fire lookout structure. The surviving cistern next to this spot probably served as an overflow tank. The northernmost palace, which probably belonged to Philetairos, was turned into a barracks for the troops whose duty must have been to protect the royal quarters.

The pavement which was discovered in one of the rooms belonging to the ruins of the palace of Eumenes II and bears the signature of the artist Hephaistion is among the earliest examples of mosaics in the true sense of the word; that is, tesserae coated with smalti were used.

Sosos of Pergamum is another mosaicist, whose works have survived to the present day in the form of Roman copies or adaptations. He is known as the creator of a particular composition known as 'asarotos oikos', or 'unswept room'. Here the artist by using artificially coloured tesserae depicted the remains of a feast on a white floor.

The mosaicists of Pergamum seem to have been among the earliest artists who superimposed one

colour on another to create an intermediate shade, such as applying a translucent coat of red plaster to white tesserae to obtain a particular bright red. They were also known as the first who reduced the size of the mosaic cubes to the size of pin-heads. By using very small mosaic cubes in graded shades of each colour they achieved gradual transitions of tone and shadow which gave their works the impression of painting.

At this point in the sightseeing tour the path leading to the storage magazines suddenly descends and gives a superb view of the dam which is built on the river Cetius (Kestel çayı). On the right side, towards the east, one can examine the best preserved portion of the Hellenistic fortifications.

During the walk along the surviving fortifications of the acropolis one can easily distinguish the sections which date back to the Hellenistic era from those built during the Byzantine period. The Hellenistic construction features large, rectangular, even-faced –and sometimes cushioned – blocks of andesite, laid in horizontal courses with vertical joints and without mortar; whereas the sections built in the later period show small stones, rubble, mixed brick and similar re-used material held together with lime mortar.

During the reign of Eumenes II the fortifications underwent extensive alterations. They were enlarged to enclose all the vulnerable spots on the west, south and east flanks. These new walls, in addition to the ones flanking the gates, featured towers at the points where the wall made a turn. The sanctuary of Demeter and the gymnasiums were also enclosed within the walls.

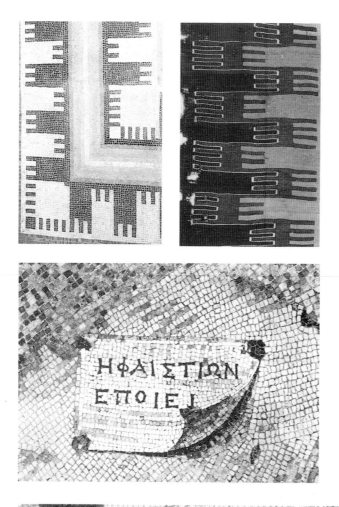

Above (left) Border detail from the mosaic signed 'Hephaistion'. First half of the second century BC. Staatliche Museen, Berlin. (right) Border detail of reciprocal combs from the nineteenth century central Anatolian kilim. 'Orient Stars' collection, Hamburg

Centre Detail from the mosaic signed 'Hephaistion'. Staatliche Museen, Berlin. In the mosaic the artist has signed his name in stone, on what looks like a casual scrap of papyrus, stuck down with blobs of red wax and dog-eared at one corner.

Below Detail from the 'unswept room'. From a villa on the Aventine. Second century. Vatican Museum, Rome. The pavement shows bird and fish bones and nutshells, as well as a scavenging mouse, and other remains lying on the floor after a banquet. Although they are part of the floor they seem to lie and cast their shadows. Thought to be a copy of the original by Sosos of Pergamum, second century BC.

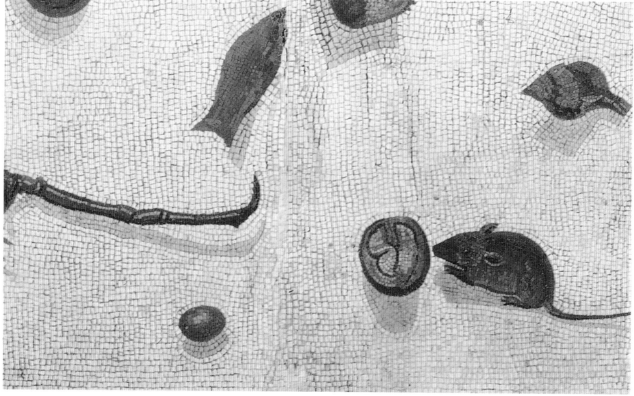

STORAGE MAGAZINES

The storage magazines of Pergamum were built at the rear part of the acropolis, on a promontory, hidden from the enemy who would approach the city from the south, and inaccessible from the surrounding plain in the other directions. These were five long and parallel constructions made of wood and resting on stone foundations which have survived to the present day. The sturdy workmanship of their substructures shows that they were designed to carry heavy loads. The vertical openings placed about a meter apart from each other helped to improve the ventilation required to preserve grain and other perishable supplies stored together with the battle gear on the upper floors. During the excavations 900 rounds of andesite shot of different calibers for catapults were discovered here and moved to the courtyard of the lower agora. They are piled on top of each other in the open area, which was the way they were kept in antiquity.

Above Andesite catapult shot discovered near the storage magazines and at present piled in the courtyard of the lower agora.

Centre Storage magazines. Stone foundations

Below Storage magazines and citadel

Those visitors who have sharp eyes can locate the surviving parts – an aqueduct and an underground channel – of a long water course which originally began at Mt Pindasos (Madra Dağı) (1150 m) – some 45 kilometers to the north – and carried water to the city. The pipeline which brought the water was made of about 240,000 pieces of conduit – each 50 to 70 cm in length – held together by perforated blocks of stone 'sleeves'. The principle on which the system applied in the final three kilometers of this course was based, is called the 'inverted siphon'. After having been collected in pools which functioned as 'loading units' the water flowed down the slope and up the other side, without appreciable loss of flow. Also, after having travelled such a long way in closed pipes it tasted flat and had to be aired; its cascading from one pool or tank to the other increased its

Aqueduct

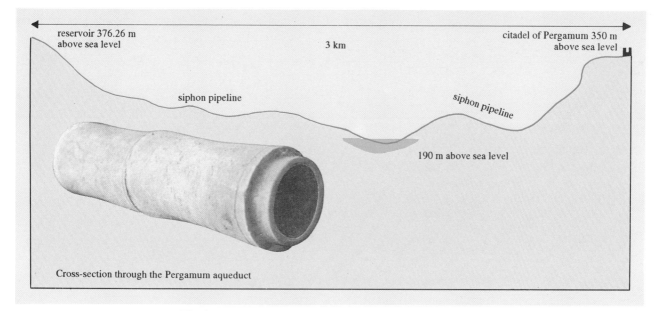

The following labels appear within the figure:

reservoir 376.26 m above sea level

3 km

citadel of Pergamum 350 m above sea level

siphon pipeline

siphon pipeline

190 m above sea level

Cross-section through the Pergamum aqueduct

The last part of the water course of Pergamum (after 'The Times Atlas of Archaeology')

sparkle and palatability and helped release its mud, pebbles and other sediments. Even contemporary engineers regard the technical problems involved in bringing water to the acropolis of Pergamum as formidable. The loading unit was 376 meters above sea level and the destination – the acropolis – was only about 350 meters above sea level.

The absence of any remains of conduits from the kingdom era may indicate that originally lead conduits were used. In addition to its intrinsic value, this metal has the advantage of being easily melted and made into something else, and thus rarely survived in its original shape. Chemical analysis of the stone beds on which the conduits were laid has shown that they contain a fifty times greater lead concentration than the normal amount found in the vicinity. During the Roman period the same water course was laid with earthenware replacements along its entire length. After it reached the big water tower located at the highest point on the citadel, the water was distributed to the palace buildings, public fountains and pools, baths, houses, and finally the sewage system. Nevertheless, the exact place where the water entered into the citadel has not yet been identified.

For the kings of Pergamum water was a crucial element of survival and both the inscriptions and the surviving ruins of aqueducts, canals and cisterns confirm the importance that they gave to supplying the city with a continuous flow of water. In the Roman era, in order to meet the requirements of a growing population and new baths, additional sources – sometimes 80 kilometers away – were utilized.

TEMPLE OF TRAJAN

The temple of Trajan is the only edifice on the citadel which is genuinely Roman. There is little left from of the buildings which occupied this area during the Hellenistic period. In order to construct the temple, the ground was levelled by building a terrace resting on an arched and vaulted substructure, in the typical Roman manner; and on this the sacred enclosure and the temple were raised. This substructure has survived until the present day in good condition. The sacred enclosure surrounding temple has stoas on three sides; the central one at the rear is higher than the others, because of the natural elevation of the rocky land. The temple itself was a peripteros (a building surrounded by columns on all sides) of the Corinthian order, featuring six columns on the short and ten on the long sides. It had a podium and a stairway (crepidoma) in the front. The frieze showed gorgon Medusa heads, and the acroteria figures of Nike.

It is thought that it was erected for Trajan (98–117) by his successor Hadrian (117–138). Heads and other pieces of the colossal marble statues of the two emperors discovered in the temple and moved to Berlin Museums, show that both of the emperors were worshipped here. Having an imperial temple would bring many visitors to a city like Pergamum during the festivals held for the imperial cult, and consequently economic benefits; thus the cities on Roman soil (including Pergamum and Ephesus) competed over building imperial temples.

Almost nothing is left of the two small monuments which once stood on the two sides of the temple and against the back wall of its sacred enclosure. The monument on the north-west side brought together the form of a pedestal for a statue and a semicircular exedra (recess) built as if for sitting. It has not survived. The monument situated symmetrically on the other side had a rectangular base made of Hellenistic material re-used during the Roman period. At present it is partly reconstructed.

Below, opposite and overleaf Temple of Trajan

Library. Detail from the north wall of the reading hall

LIBRARY

The ruins of the library of Pergamum, which is said to have once held 200,000 volumes, and was second only to the library of Alexandria, are on the left – eastern – side and were originally situated between the temple of Trajan and the northern stoa of the sanctuary of Athena. It was built during the time of Eumenes II and its fame displays the love of the Pergamene kings for culture and science.

The library consisted of three rooms and a large reading hall. It is the only Hellenistic library ruin ever discovered. At present, the walls on the south and east sides have disappeared and the interior of the rooms is visible. The holes seen on the surfaces of the two walls of the reading hall are thought to have held the hooks from which the wooden shelves containing the scrolls were hung. To protect the books from damp, the hall was surrounded by double walls and the shelves on which the boxes containing the scrolls stood were not attached to the walls but stood about 50 cm away. Excavations have shown that this Hellenistic characteristic was also used during the Roman period, such as at the library of Ephesus. The

Marble statue of Athena which stood in the reading hall of the library of Pergamum. Second century BC Antikensammlung, Berlin. It was fashioned after the statue of Athena Parthenos. The helmet had cuttings for three crests. The base preserves parts of six out of ten figures which cannot be identified.

large statue of Athena (4.5 meters), which was modelled after Athena Parthenos (work of Phidias; over 12 meters and made of gold and ivory, *c* 447–432 BC) discovered in this hall, is now in the Berlin Museum. It is obvious that a building of four rooms could not have held about 200,000 volumes, and unless this number was an exaggeration there should have been other buildings where the scrolls were kept. The end of this famous library is not known. It is said that Mark Antony – thought he did not own it – promised to give it to Cleopatra after the destruction of the library at Alexandria during Caesar's punishment of the locals in 48 BC, but it is not known if he fulfilled his promise.

The Roman writer Marcus T. Varro (*c* 116–27 BC), who lived in the city, informs us that in order to prevent the library of Pergamum from becaming too important the Ptolemaic kings of Egypt prohibited the export of papyrus; the Pergamenes then discovered the use of skin for writing and thus from their 'charta pergamene', or pergamene paper, the present day word 'parchment' is derived. The story must have been made up to compliment the cultural richness of the city during this period, otherwise it is known that parchment was being used in Anatolia and elsewhere long before, and no connection between the word 'pergamene' and Pergamum has been established. Whatever the cause of using parchment instead of papyrus, it resulted in the abandonment of the papyrus roll altogether. Being much thicker and heavier than papyrus, parchment was not suitable to roll and had to be kept as separate pages or given a paged book or codex form. This new form was more practical than the papyrus roll which the reader had to hold with one hand and unroll with the other. Even though this was a suitable way for reading, it was very difficult for research. This is thought to be the reason why ancient quotations often contain mistakes. There was also the economic advantage of using both sides of a page of codex. Both papyrus and parchment were expensive materials; nevertheless the 'page' form though it uses more space for margins seems to offer more space for actual writing.

SANCTUARY OF ATHENA

Athena was the chief goddess of Pergamum and her temple was the oldest in the city, dating back to the fourth century BC.

The sanctuary consisted of a temple, sacred enclosure, stoas on three sides and a monumental entrance. From the temple proper only some parts of its foundations—just above the theatre—have survived. At the spots where the wooden clasps held the blocks of stone together it displays marks in the shape of swallow tail. The corner stones were held together by iron clasps. It was built of trachyte, in Doric order, and surrounded by six columns on the short and ten on the long sides. A stairway of two steps surrounded it on all sides. Its altar stood on the south side. A narrow tunnel of twenty-nine steps whose lowest part is carved out of the living rock of the hill, and which is still in use, connects the temple to the theatre. The fact that the tunnel is unusually narrow has led archaeologists to think that it was reserved for the use of a few personages. Fragments of some of the columns and the architrave of the temple have been moved to the Berlin Museums. Excavations have shown that the northern half of its foundation was left under the Byzantine church which was built here in the sixth century. The marble floor of this church extending eastwards can be distinguished. The cistern situated to the south close to the remains of the Byzantine tower is thought to date from the Hellenistic period as well.

During the reign of Eumenes II, along the north and east side of the sacred enclosure, a pair of two-storeyed stoas and close to the gate of the citadel a

Sanctuary of Athena

monumental gate were added. This gate which has been restored at present in Berlin, has two storeys, the lower being Doric, and the higher one in Ionic order. The inscription on the architrave of the lower storey reads 'King Eumenes to Athena Bringer of Victory'. On the architrave of the upper storey a frieze of garlands supported by bulls heads alternating with eagles is represented. The arches of the garlands bear libation cups and owls. The balustrade is decorated with a frieze which showed the weapons taken as booty from the Galatians (oval shields), Syrians, and Macedonians (round shields). It is known that in 278 BC the Bithynian king of Nicomedia (İzmit) invited the Gauls to Anatolia, and transported some twenty thousand warriors across the straits to unruly serve him as mercenaries. These unruly warriors were to occupy the Gordion and Ancyra area and were to name this piece of Anatolia 'Galatia' after themselves.

Right, above Sanctuary of Athena. Hellenistic wooden clasp marks on the foundation blocks

Right, centre Sanctuary of Athena. Cistern

Santuary of Athena. Base of the statue of Augustus

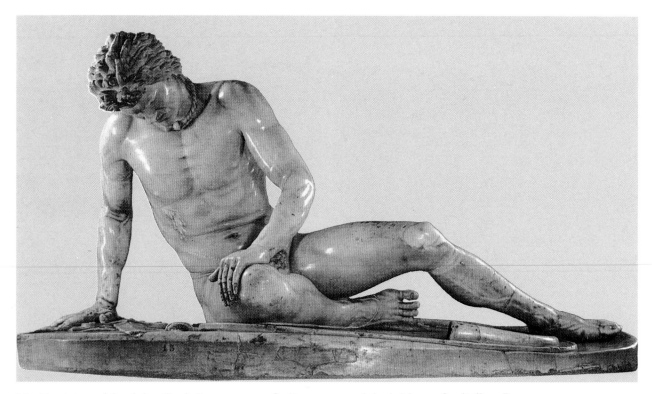

Marble statue of the dying Gaul. Roman copy of a Pergamene original. Museo Capitolino, Rome

Until this territory was incorporated in the growing Roman Republic the Gauls, or Galatians, were a continuous menace to all the nations surrounding them.

Among the monuments which decorated the sacred enclosure there was a group showing the victories of Attalos I and Eumenes II against the Galatians. The 'Dying Gaul' and another, 'Gaul Killing Himself', plunging a dagger into his chest after having killed his wife, are Roman copies of two of these.

The ruins of the round monument in the centre of the courtyard are thought to have supported first a statue of Athena, and than the bronze original of the statue of the emperor Augustus (31 BC–14 AD), whose marble copy is at present kept in the Vatican Museum.

The surviving sculpture from the period *c* 330–100 BC is characterized by a growing realism in modelling, poise and expression, and in the repertoire of the chosen subjects, a movement thought to have been initiated by the Greek sculptor Lysippos (active

c 360–315 BC). The artists of the Hellenistic period show a new interest in subjects such as old age, deformity, childhood, or anger and despair, subjects which were rarely dealt with until then, and they tried to represent the movements of the human body in different contrasting directions, the texture and folds of dress and human character and emotion.

One of the styles distinguished in this new movement has been characterized by 'marked contrasts in the various planes, closely knit groups, lively action with frequent contortions and emotional expressions' and has been called 'Pergamene'. The sculptures dedicated by the kings of Pergamum were among the finest examples of this particular style of the Hellenistic art.

Opposite Monumental gate of the sanctuary of Athena. Pergamum Museum, Berlin. The inscription on the lower architrave reads in Greek *BASILEUS EUMENES ATHENAI NIKEPHOROI*, or 'King Eumenes to Athena Bringer of Victory'.

Marble relief of a hero from Pergamum. End of third–beginning of second centuries BC. Istanbul Archaeological Museums

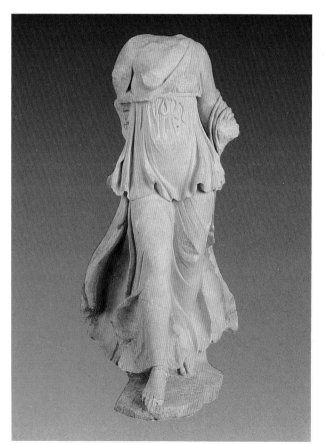

Marble statue of Nike from Pergamum. End of second century BC. Istanbul Archaeological Museums

THEATRE

One of the most impressive edifices of Pergamum was its theatre. Though it could take no more than 10,000 spectators, the deep and wide valley extending in front of it, and its architectural setting, with the other buildings on the higher ground placed fan–wise above it, made it probably the most attractive theatre – and at present makes it the most charming theatre ruin – in western Anatolia. It is known as the steepest theatre of the ancient world.

The theatre dates back to the foundation days of the kingdom, and probably took its present form during the time of Eumenes II. In the Roman era performances were moved to the new theatre and the amphitheatre built on the plain, and a stone podium – still visible – to serve as a speaker's platform was constructed in the orchestra. The surviving impressive remains above the seats belong to a Byzantine tower.

The part reserved for the spectators (auditorium) had 80 rows of seats made of andesite and in order to facilitate exit and entry was divided into three sections by two horizontal landings (diazoma). The king's box, which was made of marble, was located above the centre of the lowest landing. The rows of large square holes seen at the centre of the theatre terrace held the wooden supports of the low stage building on which the actors played (proskenion) and the background stage building (skene) itself. After the performances, the portable stage was dismantled, and stored in the lower floors below the supporting wall of the theatre terrace, and the holes would have been closed with stone plaques. In this manner, the terrace would become available for people who might wish to take a walk here.

At the beginning the Greek theatre consisted of

Theatre

only a chorus, a group of men who did the singing and dancing in the circular area called the orchestra, literally the dancing floor. Later an actor was introduced to exchange dialogue with the leader of the chorus. As the number of actors increased a higher place became necessary in order to hear their voices better. All the performers were men. Women's parts were also played by men, wearing masks. These painted masks served to identify characters and showed the age and feelings of the actors as well. Also, actors could change masks quickly and represent different persons. The large and open mouth of a mask would amplify the actor's voice. Happy characters wore bright colours and tragic ones dark colours. In the later period the colour of drapery and the way it was worn would come to express the nationality or status of the actor.

A minimal admission charge was applied at the entrance. Often the fees of poor people would be paid by the state or rich citizens. Some citizens had the right of free admission and reserved seats. The plays would last all day and the audience usually brought food — mostly snacks such as figs, raisins or nuts — and wine. After the performance prizes would be given to the successful writers, chief actors or those citizens who were responsible for meeting the expenses of performances. While the actor of the day would become the hero of the day, spectators might once in a while come to blows over the comparative merits of rival actors.

Theatre and Temple of Trajan

Opposite Theatre. Byzantine tower

TEMPLE OF DIONYSUS

The temple of Dionysus is among the best preserved ruins of ancient Pergamum. Its location, being so close to the theatre where festivals, spectacles, and music contests were held, is most appropriate to the god worshipped here. The original temple of the third century BC was built of andesite, and during the reign of the Roman Emperor Caracalla (211–217), underwent extensive restoration in marble, becoming a prostyle of Ionic order approached by a stairway of twenty-five steps. Its altar has survived. It is known that for some time the Emperor stayed in Pergamum and was worshipped here under the name of 'New Dionysus' in gratitude for the services he had done for the city. Nevertheless, it is said that when he visited the Asclepion for treatment through dreams, the healer-god was unmoved and did not send him any dreams.

The theatre terrace runs for about 250 m between the temple of Dionysus and the double-arched entrance which once existed at its south end. It was flanked by a long stoa on the west, overlooking the plain and a shorter one which started after the theatre on the land (east) side. The small building which was situated between the theatre and the beginning of the east stoa is thought to have been used as a special sanctuary by the congregation of the performers.

Even if one walks down to the temple of Dionysus, the most convenient way to continue sightseeing is to leave the theatre by its middle landing and walk towards the altar of Zeus.

Opposite Temple of Dionysus and valley of Selinus

Temple of Dionysus

ALTAR OF ZEUS

The altar of Zeus was the largest and most impressive edifice of Hellenistic Pergamum. The oldest information about this extraordinary edifice comes from the *Book of Memorable Facts* of Lucius Ampelius, a Roman citizen who described the altar about four hundred years after it was built: 'At Pergamum is a great marble altar, forty feet high, with remarkable statues, and the entirety is surrounded by a Battle of the Giants'. This was a very popular theme of the Greek repertoire of fine arts. It commemorated the Greek victory over the Persians, over their enemies in general, and symbolized the victory of order over chaos in bolder terms. For the Attalid rulers, it was a visual representation of their victory over the Galatians, and other enemies. After this, and until 1871, when the German engineer Carl Human, who was then supervising construction firm in Turkey, informed the Berlin Museums that he came across reliefs of 'a battle with men, horses, wild animals', there is no mention of the monument in the written records.

The German excavation began in 1878 and lasted about four years. By the time it was concluded a grand collection of 97 relief panels of the Gigantomachy together with 2,000 fragments, 35 panels related to Telephus frieze and 100 fragments, plus numerous statues, inscriptions, busts and other architectural material had been uncovered. At present the altar of Zeus is situated in a restored state in Berlin.

The entrance to the terrace on which it was built was on the eastern side from the main street. The

Base of the altar of Zeus

Altar of Zeus. Pergamum Museum, Berlin

monument is made of marble and measures 36.44 x 34.20 meters. It begins with a five-stepped stairway which surrounds it on all sides. On top of this, a horseshoe-shaped podium encircled by a frieze measuring 2.30 x 120 meters stands. On the open (west) side a wide flight of stairs leads to a colonnade of Ionic columns which surrounds the high podium on three sides, as well. At the centre of the open place located behind the colonnade there is an altar for burnt offerings. The animals were sacrificed in front of the stairs and the parts reserved for gods were later burned on the altar of offerings. The surface of the walls around this altar is covered with another smaller frieze. The roof of the monument is decorated with centaurs, quadrigas (four-horse chariots), teams of horses and figures of gods.

The large frieze which encircles the podium depicts the mythical battle between the Greek gods and the Giants. The latter are creatures born from the sky and earth mother Gaia. Their physique is characterized by long locks and beards, and serpent-tails for feet. When Zeus confines their brothers, the Titans, in Tartarus, they are enraged and all of a sudden attack the Olympian gods. Hera prophesies that unless a lion-skinned mortal joins the fight, the Giants cannot be killed. Heracles takes his place near his father Zeus and all the Giants are killed.

The minor frieze which surrounded the three walls of the room of the altar of offerings carried a single undivided composition depicting episodes from the life of Telephus, Heracles' son and founder of Pergamum.

If the large frieze, which actually commemorates the victory of Attalids over the Galatians and in doing this includes Heracles, the father of the founder of their city, and the small frieze, which relates the story of the founder, are seen together the altar of Zeus becomes a visual display of noble descendancy of the Attalids.

Neither the paint which once covered the bluish marble, nor the gold and bronze accessories of goddesses have survived. While the names of gods and goddesses were indicated above each relief, at the bottom the names of Giants and the sculptors were shown. Although only a few of the names, such as Menecrates, Dionysiades, Orestes and Theorrhetos can be distinguished from the surviving fragments, the sculptors are thought to have been from Pergamum and Athens. The quality of the work indicates that they must have been the master builders and sculptors of the period.

Right Marble relief from the eastern frieze of the altar of Zeus. First half of the second century BC. Pergamum Museum, Berlin. Zeus, accompanied by his sacred animal, an eagle, fights the leader of the giants, Porphyrion, and another younger Giant. The father of the gods is depicted holding a shield (aegis) in his left hand and thunderbolts in the other. His shield seems to have been decorated with snakes. A thunderbolt has hit the right shoulder of the young giant who is shown in agony and holding his wound with his left hand. The old Giant has raised his arm bearing a shield of lion pelt to defend himself. The eagle of Zeus is shown attacking one of the snake-heads of the tails of the Giant at his nostrils.

Preceeding pages Marble relief from the eastern frieze of altar of Zeus. First half of the second century BC. Pergamum Museum, Berlin. The left part shows the triple-bodied Hecate, goddess of ways, witchcraft and magic, accompanied by her Molossian dog and the Giant Klytios. Hecate is clad in a rich garment with plenty of deep folds. Her other two bodies are rendered in the background. Having taken a forward step, she is seen trying to burn the Giant with a torch. The naked and bearded Giant is about to hurl a large boulder held with his two hands above his head. His feet have snake heads and one of these has fixed its teeth on the shield of the goddess. In the background her two other arms are shown holding a lance and a sword. The rest of the picture shows a naked and armed Giant (Otos?) facing Artemis who is armed with bow and arrow. She wears a short chiton typical for a huntress. Her bow is stretched towards the young Giant who is represented opposite her standing with a drawn sword. Under her feet is the corpse of Giant she has already killed. Between the two and again on the ground is a third Giant who has been bitten by her dog on his neck. The Giant has raised his right arm and is seen trying to pluck out the eyes of the animal with his hand. His other carefully worked hand rests on the boot of the goddess. One of the heads of his snake tails has fixed its teeth on the dress of Hecate.

Right Marble relief of dancing maenad from Pergamum. second century BC. Istanbul Archaeological Museums

Below Upper agora

UPPER AGORA

The upper agora, or the 'state' agora of Pergamum occupied the terrace to the south and immediately below the altar of Zeus. Except for the remains of an apsidal building in its north-west corner, which are of the Roman era, all the ruins date back to the late Hellenistic period. On three sides the market place was surrounded with stoas as far as the terrace would allow. These were single-storeyed on the side facing the courtyard of the agora. A basement of storage rooms had to be added to the stoa on the south side

Right Grave of Carl Humann (1839–1896) who discovered the altar of Zeus

Below Upper agora. Marble fragments

because of the sloping of the land. Their columns were Doric and only the upper two-thirds was fluted. These are thought to have kept their original form until the eighth century when they were dismantled to be used to build the Byzantine fortifications. The floor of the courtyard was laid with trachyte. The temple of the market was on the west side. It was of the type called prostyle (preceded by a porch with columns in front) with antae (projecting walls on two sides). The edifice had four columns in the front which were of a strange mixed order, and was probably dedicated to Hermes, god of merchants.

The ancient main street entered the market square from the south and left it in the opposite direction, and passing by the gates of the altar of Zeus and the heroon, climbed up towards the citadel gate (today's entrance).

The sightseeing tour of the citadel of Pergamum terminates here. On the way to the exit by the ramp of the main street and just before walking out of the agora, a conscientious visitor may notice the large granite block situated on the right – east – side under which Carl Humann, who discovered the altar of Zeus, rests. The traveller who would like to visit the rest of the acropolis of Pergamum, known as the middle acropolis and lower acropolis, should continue walking down the ancient main street.

The edifices in the citadel were under the close control of the royal family, members of the noble classes and the military dignitaries, and they gave this section of the city a sacred and austere atmosphere. The middle and lower acropolis with their own group of sanctuaries, gymnasiums, agora and other buildings of more social character were cosmopolitan places which members of the lower classes frequented without any hindrance from the ruling class in the citadel.

Opposite Marble statue of Hermaphrodite from Pergamum. Second century BC. Istanbul Archaeological Museums

MAIN STREET

After this point the visitor begins to walk on the ancient main street. It is paved with andesite blocks which sometimes become as large as 0.5 x 1 meters in size. It begins at the gate of the citadel and coils down through the most important public buildings of the city like a giant snake. First, it goes by the entrances of the altar of Zeus and the heroon, and crosses the upper agora. It descends sharply through the residential quarters and turns to the east by forty-five degrees above the terrace on which the sanctuary of Hera Basileia was built. Turning sharply in the opposite direction near the east fortifications, it continues downwards by the public fountain (close to the vaulted stairway of the middle gymnasium), the lower agora and the house of consul Attalos, reaching the gate of Eumenes.

Main street, theatre and Temple of Trajan

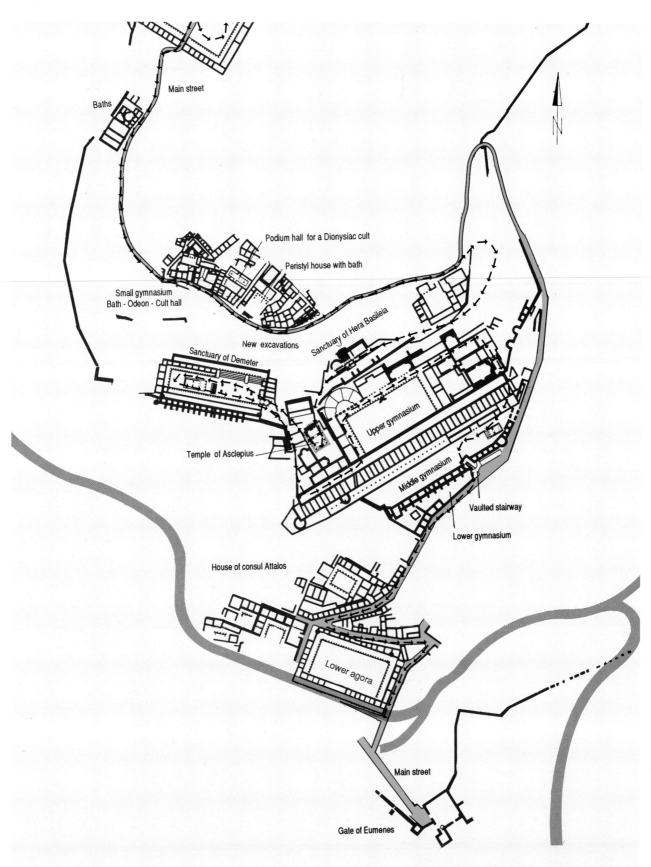

Plan of middle and lower acropolis

MIDDLE ACROPOLIS
RESIDENTIAL BUILDINGS

The excavations carried out in the section between the citadel and the public buildings, such as the sanctuary of Demeter or the upper gymnasium of the middle acropolis, have shown that this area was occupied with buildings related to the daily city life and was built over during the Hellenistic, Roman and Byzantine periods. The excavations were aimed at clearing the area of its Byzantine rubble which was mostly re-used material, and revealing the original Hellenistic and Roman character of the buildings.

Baths

The first group of ruins, situated on the right — western — side of the main street after a short walk belonged to a bath building. Except for the round tepidarium, which has a wide recess, the rest of the rooms are indistinguishable. While the ruins are from

Residential area. Baths. Cistern

the Roman period, the remains of a floor mosaic discovered here point to the existence of a Hellenistic structure as well.

Small gymnasium (bath – odeon – cult hall)

The second group of ruins encountered on the opposite – eastern – side of the main street belong to a small gymnasium which consisted of a bath complex, an odeon and a cult hall. While the last two parts were originally Hellenistic, the baths were added during the Roman period. The gymnasium is thought to have been used until the end of the fourth century, undergoing various alterations throughout its history.

The side street climbing uphill just before the baths led to a public latrine, connected to the baths. The drainage channel running under this narrow street emptied into the main sewage system which runs under the main street.

Roman latrines were usually built close to the baths because the best way of disposing the water yielded by the latter was to allow it to flow continuously into the latrine sewer. As was the case

Residential buildings. Small gymnasium. Baths

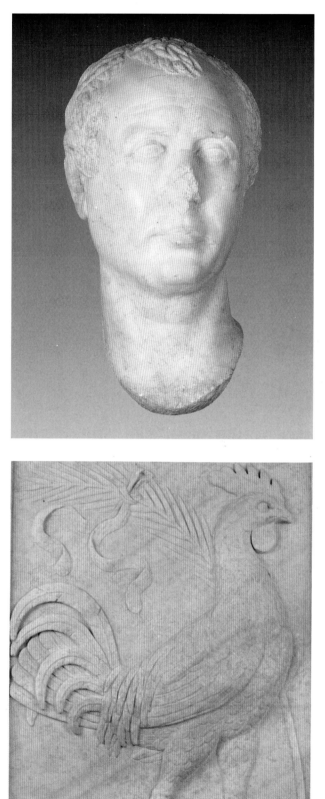

with the baths, a small fee was necessary at the latrine. A Roman latrine was not divided into individual cubicles, and no embarrassment was felt by the people who shared it. It was a common experience to come across a friend here, chat and invite him for dinner. The continuous running water which was channelled from the baths took the waste away. There was no toilet paper, but a piece of sponge attached to the end of a stick which could be washed in the narrow channel running along the rim of the arc of the seats on the floor and emptied into the main sewer, was used. Hand-washing was done in marble or stone basins. In some of the Roman latrines a flushing system was built at the middle point of the circle of the seats. Here the water collected in a basin could be flushed below or into the open narrow channel in the front. The floor was usually mosaic paved, and the centre was occupied by a graceful pool with fountains or statues.

The main entrance of the baths was from the main street. Originally the surviving columned courtyard was preceded by a flight of steps which no longer exist. An exit on the eastern side probably led to the uppermost row of seats of the odeon. Above the apsidal frigidarium and to the north, there was once a water tank. Further north a second water reservoir can be distinguished by its plastered brick walls and waterproof floor. The highest point of the site offers a full view of the complex. The furnace and the sweat-bath (laconicium) in the form of a small round room are situated at the south of the courtyard. Access to the stoking room (praefernium), simultaneously used for storing wood, was from the main street.

Marble relief with lance and sword from small gymnasium. First century. Bergama Museum

Between the baths and the odeon there was a small hallway with steps which was succeeded by three small rooms thought to have served as a kitchen and pantry where the cult meals were prepared. The seats of the small odeon are arranged in segments of concentric circles probably to make best use of the limited space. Originally the odeon and the cult hall were preceded by a forecourt with two deep cisterns below it.

The following part of gymnasium was a heroon, dedicated by the people of Pergamum to a person whose head was discovered in front of the cult apse and is at present on display in Bergama Museum. He is known as one Diodoros Pasparos, a citizen of high status in the city in about 70 BC. The surviving reliefs in the cult hall are thought to date from the period following the big earthquake of 17, after which the building and its decoration were restored.

Originally the hall was decorated with eighteen relief panels which were placed symmetrically (two times the same nine motifs) on each side of the central niche. The surviving reliefs, whose originals have been moved to Bergama Museum, show a victorious cock, a helmet and the star of the Dioscuri, and a sword and a lance. One of the finds was a phallus relief carved on a stone block. This block is now built into the front of the new wall at the right (south) side.

Marble relief with helmet from small gymnasium. First century. Bergama Museum

Dining house

Excavations have shown that along the east wall of the marble hall a dining house of three rooms existed: a room on the street with a grate cut into the rock of the floor, a dining room with walls bearing murals and a third room with a large grate partially cut into the rock. The diggings in this last room have revealed bones of pig, partridge, chicken and suchlike.

Wine or oil shop

The third room after the marble hall has large holes in its floor into which the large baked clay jars (pithoi) which must have contained oil or wine were sunk. Its entrance was close to one of the side walls. Originally the construction is thought to have had wide counters facilitating the sale, and opening onto the street between piers joined by a low wall.

Residential buildings. Dining house and wine or oil shop

Podium hall for a Dionysiac cult

The area at the back of the structures which were connected with eating, drinking and shopping was occupied by a large hall measuring some 24 x 10 meters.

The large terrace which stood in front of the hall on the eastern side contained a fountain and a deep pit cut into the living rock of the hill. The entrance of the hall was located between the fountain and the pit. The niche for the cult image was opposite the entrance. The altar and the remains of murals depicting Dionysiac cult practices found in the niche have been moved to Bergama Museum.

The hall is named by archaeologists after the high and large podium which encircles its walls. Access to the podium was by narrow stairways. The narrow marble slab (at present restored in concrete) which ran along the edge of the podium is thought to have been used for serving food on it. The adherents of the cult are thought to have lain on the large podium during the cult ceremonies, while the walls were covered with paintings showing cult objects and motifs encircled in simple panels.

The fountain, the deep pit, and the podium give the impression that an Oriental and Dionysiac cult must have been celebrated here. This idea is strengthened by the decoration of the hall which was modest, appropriate to the believers in such a cult that would have been popular with middle class people such as merchants or shopkeepers. It is thought to have been built in the second century when Eastern cults were very much in fashion in the Roman world, and used until the fourth century.

The peristyle house with bath

Like the rest of the buildings the house is situated on the north-eastern side of the main street. Some of its columns dating back to the Hellenistic period have been erected at their original spots. During the Roman period the house was enlarged and a heated private bath was added. The large water reservoir belonged to this addition.

At this point the main street makes a turn in the

Residential buildings. Podium hall for a Dionysial cult

eastern direction and continues to descend gently. After this point both sides of the main street are crowded with ruins. These belonged to residences built out of the available, often second hand material in the area, and without any planning. While the area on the left has been cleared of its Byzantine superstructure, excavations in the opposite slope still continue.

On the left side there are the ruins of some stores and workshops. The upper levels of these constructions and the ruins occupying the area in the background served as residences. One striking feature of this area is the abundance of cisterns.

Among these ruins the one with a large stone arch – partly reconstructed – built over a rock-cut cistern is thought to have served as a public water house.

The last group of ruins on the opposite (southern) side of the main street is thought to be the Megalesion of Pergamum where the cult of Cybele, or the Great Mother, was worshipped. Its large columned courtyard was surrounded with halls on four sides, and one of the rooms built at the back of the east hall served as the cult room. In the Roman period the north hall was replaced by a state room (exedra). During the later centuries the halls were divided into smaller units which served as workshops, and a large water reservoir was built below the courtyard. In the fifth–sixth centuries and twelfth–fourteenth centuries two churches following each other were built on the cult room as well.

After a short walk one leaves the main street and turning in the opposite direction towards the west, walks into the street leading to the terrace on which the sanctuary of Hera Basileia is built.

Residential buildings. Peristyle house with bath

51

Opposite, above Residential buildings. Rock-cut cistern

Opposite, below Residential buildings. Remains of a Hellenistic house

Right Sanctuary of Hera Basileia. Stairway and gabled pediment

Below Marble statue from the sanctuary of Hera Basileia. second century BC. Istanbul Archaeological Museums. The statue is thought to represent Zeus or Attalos II.

SANCTUARY OF HERA BASILEIA

The sanctuary of Hera Basileia faces south and dominates the area above the upper gymnasium. The location chosen for it indicates that it was meant to be seen easily, and from long distances. The temple is flanked by a semicircular exedra in the west and a stoa in the east. These buildings and the temple are erected on a higher terrace than the altar. The andesite wall which is surrounding the sacred precinct has survived until the present day in good condition.

The temple was of the type known as prostyle, and in Doric order, with four columns at the front. Its long stairway of twelve steps was flanked by balustrades. Its visible parts, such as the porch (pronaos) were built of marble, less visible parts bore marble facing, and those hidden from view were of andesite. The inscriptions on the surviving pieces of its architrave were found sufficient to learn that the building was commissioned on the orders of Attalos II, who dedicated it to Hera Basileia. The headless statue which was discovered in its inner chamber (naos) is thought to belong to this king or Zeus, the husband of Hera (Istanbul Archaeological Museums).

The function of the semicircular exedra and the stoa which flanked the temple is not known. In the stoa, a couch (podium) with a three-stepped stairway has survived.

The ruins which occupy the area west of the sanctuary of Hera are thought to belong to the town hall (prytaneion).

SANCTUARY OF DEMETER

The sanctuary of Demeter occupies a large rectangular terrace overlooking the modern town of Bergama. During the reign of Philetarios it was outside the city walls. In order to reach the sanctuary originally people approached it from the direction of gymnasium and first entered a square which had a fountain and a sacrificial pit, both being closely connected with the cult of Demeter which required plenty of ritual cleansing, offerings, and sacrifices. The square was followed by a stairway of five steps, a two-columned monumental gate, and another flight of ten steps. The inscription found on the frieze of the architrave of this entrance states that the building of the stoas and the *oikoi* (large sitting rooms) was commissioned by Apollonis of Cyzicus, the wife of Attalos I.

On the left (south side) of the sanctuary there was a long stoa of two aisles formed by a row of columns

Sanctuary of Demeter

Reconstruction of capital from the inner colonnade of the upper storey of the stoa of Attalos II in Athens. Mid–second century BC

Sanctuary of Demeter. Aeolic or 'leaf capital'. *c* 200 BC. These capitals, and similar ones, which have survived in the stoa of Attalos in Athens, show that the Attalids wanted to establish a Pergamene tradition by choosing a local capital form.

on each side. The basement of the outer aisle has survived to the present day in good condition. During the Roman period this part became a stronghold in the city walls.

The other side of the sanctuary was divided into two parts. While the western half had a stoa, in the other half – close to the entrance – ten rows of seats which could hold about 800 spectators were built, to accommodate participants during the cult ceremonies. Demeter was the Earth-goddess, the goddess of nature and all plants. When her daughter Persephone was kidnapped by Hades, the King of Tartaros (the god of the underworld), she was the cause of a dreadful year for mankind; seeds would not sprout, flowers would not blossom, and no fruit would grow. Zeus had to ask his brother Hades to release Persephone and in the end it was decided that she should remain one-third of the year underground, when it is winter, and two-thirds of the year above ground, when she comes up again bringing the spring and summer. A relief of Roman period depicting Demeter with a torch in one hand and the rope of a sacrificial animal in the other, standing beside the altar was discovered in the

sanctuary and at present is displayed in Bergama Museum. Her cult promised an inner meaning to life and a happier afterlife, and was very popular with people, especially women.

Above this and extending all along the sanctuary there was another stoa whose rear wall has survived in its entire length. At the end of the sanctuary there were four rooms, probably some of the *oikoi* mentioned in the inscription of Queen Apollonis. It is thought that the rooms built at the east end of the sanctuary were also among the rooms referred to as *oikoi*.

The temple and its large altar – both in andesite – were situated in the western half of the sanctuary somewhat off the east-west axis and close to the south side, probably to give the spectators in the north stoa a clear view of the ceremonies which took place here. The temple was Ionic and in antis. While some of the surviving inscriptions show that both edifices were erected by Philetairos, and his younger brother Eumenes (the father of King Eumenes I), in memory of their mother, Boa of Paphlagonia, there are those showing that they were restored – turned into a Corinthian prostyle by the addition of marble columns and a pediment – in the mid–second century by Claudius Silianus Aesimus, a member of the famous Siliani family of Pergamum. The pediment of this latter construction stands by the temple. The Hellenistic altar is fairly large and was, originally, decorated with elegant volutes at its corners. At the centre of the sanctuary the remains of several more altars can be seen.

The surviving inscriptions inform us that while the temple and the altar in the beginning were devoted solely to the worship of Demeter, by Apollonis' time Persephone, the daughter of Demeter, was also included in the repertoire. After the restoration in the Roman era it was again dedicated to Demeter Karpophoros and Persephone.

UPPER GYMNASIUM

The gymnasium (from Greek 'gymnos'; naked) was probably the most magnificent complex of Pergamum and at present is known as the largest and most complete of its kind which has survived from antiquity. It was built on three terraces and consisted of the upper gymnasium for young men, the middle gymnasium for adolescent boys, and the lower gymnasium reserved for children. All the buildings of the gymnasium date back to the days of the kingdom but have undergone extensive alterations during the Roman centuries, the upper gymnasium most of all. While the surviving marble pieces and remains of vaults and walls made in stone or brick with mortar, which once bore marble or hewn-stone facing, are from the Roman period, the andesite remains indicate a Hellenistic origin.

Sanctuary of Demeter. East gate from the courtyard

Right, above Sanctuary of Demeter. Basement of south stoa

Centre, right Sanctuary of Demeter. Roman pediment

Centre, left Sanctuary of Demeter. Roman altars

Right, below Sanctuary of Demeter. Hellenistic temple

Left, below Sanctuary of Demeter. Hellenistic altar

The actual upper gymnasium complex, which was reserved for young men, consisted of a large courtyard surrounded with stoas on all sides, and bath buildings in the west and east. In addition to its principal entrance, which was from the main street on the eastern side, it was accessible from the middle gymnasium by various narrow and simple stairways. Its courtyard was of earth and used for exercises. Pentathlon, discus, jumping, javelins, wrestling, boxing, weight lifting, and ball playing were only some of the activities held here.

The buildings which belonged to gymnasium began with the temple of Asclepios which is situated above the western terrace. This small temple happens to have been the only purely Hellenistic edifice in the upper gymnasium. Except for the remains of its marble blocks nothing has survived of the temple. It was a prostyle temple in Doric order, and archaeological research has shown that the monument which was built in the first half of the second century BC, saw extensive restoration while it was in the building process becoming Ionic order. The torso probably belonging to the healer-god Asclepios found here led archaeologists to think that the edifice was dedicated to this god. The area sloping down towards the south on this side of the courtyard was occupied with buildings related to baths both during the Hellenistic and Roman periods. Some of the buildings seem to have been used as cisterns during the Byzantine centuries. Of the three rooms situated in the west stoa, the function of the first is not known. The second was a bathroom. The seven marble bath-tubs surviving in this room are wash-basins. The room must obviously have served to clean the body

Upper gymnasium. West baths and courtyard

after physical exercise or competitions. The third room was used as a small salon attached to the odeon which could seat about one thousand spectators. This originally roofed theatre has no orchestra, and thus is thought to have been used for musical contests, or for lectures or meetings. Although athletic institutions, gymnasiums are known to have attached importance to musical training.

The most important room around the courtyard, where all major events took place, occupied the middle part of the north stoa. An inscription found on an architrave piece indicates that the room next to it was reserved for the cult of the Emperor. The quality of the marble fittings of this room give the impression that special importance was given to its decoration.

The most impressive group of ruins in the upper gymnasium are those of its Roman baths. Baths or 'thermae' were an indispensable luxury of the Roman way of life and from the very early period of Greek medicine doctors prescribed bathing as a means of curing illness and maintaining health. While the palaestra of the gymnasium exercised the body, thermae cleansed it. In addition to this, baths - like agoras - were social centres where people met friends, chatted and heard the latest news. The wealthy citizens had their private baths in their houses; the rest of the people used the public baths. They were leased by individuals and thus a nominal fee was applied. Children were free. While there were baths which were run by the state free of charge, sometimes rich citizens were held responsible for the expenses of baths. For men and women the same buildings would be used but different hours were assigned and announced by the ringing of a bell.

Upper gymnasium. Temple of Asclepius

A typical Roman bath consisted of four parts. First, the bather entered the dressing-room or apodyterium. Often there would be an intermediate dry sweat-bath (without a hot water pool) after this. Next he proceeded to the caldarium, where the temperature was warm and where he could sprinkle steaming hot water from a large tub or pool on his body and scrape the dust, sweat and the ceroma (an unguent of oil and wax which made the skin more supple) if he came from exercise, with a metal strigil. The steam and temperature of the room were controlled by an opening in the ceiling above the hot water pool. It was very difficult to rub oneself properly and an assistant was necessary. Cleansed and dried, the third step was tepidarium where one could cool off gradually. Finally one would take a plunge in the cold pool of the frigidarium. While wealthy visitors would have their personal physicians or slaves for massage, there would be free-lance masseurs or trainers for hire as well. Manicure or 'unwanted hair removal' services were also available.

The baths stood at the back of the east stoa. Although nothing has survived of the marble facing of their walls, these baths are still as impressive as they must have been during the time that they were used. Some rooms display their old heating (hypocaust) system featuring circular andesite stones shaped like rough columns under the floor. This is the only example where stone was used instead of brick for such supports, probably because in Pergamum there was a lot of fireresistant andesite stone at hand.

There is nothing left of the south stoa. Nevertheless,

Upper gymnasium. Wash-room

Upper gymnasium

its long running track, referred to as the 'basement stadium' (from 'stade', Greek measure of distance, about 200 meters), which lay below it and was used in winter or hot summer, has survived until the present day in good condition. It was lit by the holes in its south wall. These windows are narrow on the outside, and widen inwards through the thickness of the wall, similar to the kind of slits used for shooting arrows. The surviving structures show that after a period of time its front was sealed off and it was used only for storing goods. During the late Roman period, like the sanctuary of Demeter, the upper gymnasium was also incorporated in the defense system of the city.

Upper gymnasium

MIDDLE GYMNASIUM

The middle gymnasium, which still retains its Hellenistic character, occupies the terrace below the upper gymnasium. It was reserved for the youths. On the landward side and along its entire length there was a large stoa as an upper storey, above other rooms on remaining rocky areas. The eastern part the ground floor of this stoa was divided into rooms. An inscription discovered in the sixth room, named 'exedra' by the archaeologists, has shown that the room was dedicated in Roman times to the cult of the Emperor and to the worship of Hermes and Heracles, both being gods related to physical prowess. The architecture of the small temple on the terrace was of the type of a 'templum in antis' (with its entrance section receding into the building). It was built originally in the Ionic order. In late-Hellenistic times it was altered into a Corinthian prostyle. On the surviving pieces of the temple walls, names of boys from both the Roman and the Hellenistic eras have been discovered.

Vaulted stairway

The vault-covered stairway which was the main entrance into the middle gymnasium from the main street, is one of the most impressive ruins surviving from the late Hellenistic city. It is also known as one of the oldest and from the technical point of view most interesting arch-and-vault constructions of the eastern Greek world and one of the rare cases where

Opposite, above Upper gymnasium. East baths, courtyard and the town of Bergama

Opposite, below left Upper gymnasium. Basement stadium. Staircase ascending to the courtyard

Opposite, below right Upper gymnasium. Basement stadium

Middle gymnasium. Stoa, temple, fortifications and the town of Bergama

the stone-cutters of the Hellenistic world dared to try their skill at barrel-vault. The workmanship of its builders manifests itself in the fashioning of the walls and the vaulting, displayed in the originality of the intersection of the arches at varying heights as they cover the winding stairway.

Originally, this vaulted stairway opened into a curvilinear courtyard which had two doors, one leading to the lower gymnasium and another to the main street. The marks of the two stone uprights of the frame of this second door are still visible. A section of the curving wall on the west side, adjoining to the wall of the stairway has survived.

The area on the east of the vaulted stairway was occupied by a long (21 m) and wide (3.15 m) rectangular public fountain. Its rear wall is partly survived, adjoining the stairway. Two blocks which belonged to its front wall have been set up in their original spots. This front wall was low enough for people to obtain water by lowering their buckets into the pool. The inner surface of the two stones blocks which have been put into place by the archaeologists are worn away where the vessels must have touched. Twelve columns placed in the pool carried a roof of 3 meters in height.

LOWER GYMNASIUM

The lower gymnasium, which was reserved for children, was built on the lower and narrower terrace to the north of the main street below the middle gymnasium. In order to prevent it from collapsing on the main street five box-like compartments without doors were built and filled with rubble. Nevertheless, on this side neither the rooms, nor the terrace has survived. On the opposite (north) side, a similar 'box-compartment' support of the middle terrace

Opposite Lower acropolis. Vaulted stairway and Byzantine tower

Lower acropolis. Middle gymnasium

Left Lower and middle gymnasium and Byzantine tower
Below Lower gymnasium. Supporting buttresses

was reinforced by vertical buttresses which have partly survived to the present. In the fourth recess of this buttressed wall a large stele bearing the names of the ephebes (young athletes) of the year 147 BC - the reign of Attalos II - has been discovered.

Here the main street gets as wide as five meters, and in some places it displays ancient repairwork, drainage and canals, and grooves caused by chariot wheels. As one goes down the street on the right side there are the ruins of a group of shops. The Roman copy of the herm of the Athenian sculptor Alkamenes (Istanbul Archaeological Museums) was discovered in one of these rooms, and is thought to have fallen from the house of the consul Attalos, which stood above the shops.

LOWER ACROPOLIS
HOUSE OF THE CONSUL ATTALOS

In plan this house was similar to the palaces of the Pergamene kings which were in the citadel: a courtyard surrounded with two-storeyed stoas on four sides. The rooms of various sorts were situated behind the stoas. While the lower storey was of andesite and Doric, the upper one was of marble and Ionic. The largest room of the complex, which was intended for meetings or banquets, was on the western side. By the entrance of this room stood a herm which probably bore a bronze portrait-bust of the owner of this fashionable house. An inscription carved on the front of this herm, stated that the owner of the house was Attalos, and that he was a consul, and invites his guests to share his joy in life.

A large Hellenistic cistern is located in the courtyard. A water tunnel built in later times cut into the rock, connects the cistern to the fountain situated in the lower agora. Some of the living and sleeping quarters have revealed precious Hellenistic mosaic pavements and Roman murals.

LOWER AGORA

It seems that by the beginning of the reign of Eumenes II, the location and character of the upper agora did not meet the requirements of a growing cosmopolitan city and it became necessary to build a second agora near the plain. This lower agora, which covered an area of 80 x 50 meters and was surrounded with two-storeyed stoas in Doric order, would soon become the centre of commercial life in Pergamum. The sloping of land in the south made necessary the addition of a basement floor on this side and the rooms on this side were accessible from the main street as well.

In its general outline this was a typical Hellenistic agora. The shops were situated behind the columns of the stoas which protected people from the rain in winter and too much sun in summer. Across the front some shops would have had counters on which baked clay pottery and luxury items were sold. The principal economic and social units of the kingdom were villages. Farmers who came to sell their products such as vegetables, fruit, eggs, almonds, olives and similar goods would set their stalls at the centre of the marketplace. Meat and fish were often displayed on marble slabs. Woman – except very old ladies who did not have anybody to go shopping for them – were not allowed into the marketplace. The shopping was done by male slaves. There were officials to check weights, control the blackmarket and the quality of goods. At one corner money changers would have their tables. These would also act as bankers, giving money with interest or finding profitable ventures to invest in. Men who were looking for jobs would gather in a specific area and wait for employers.

The fountain in the courtyard was supplied from the large cistern under the courtyard of consul Attalos which occupied the higher ground above the agora. The agora would usually have other graceful monuments, statues of politicians or athletes. The inscribed tablets discovered in the agora have given detailed information about the regulations for

Lower acropolis. East fortifications

Opposite Lower acropolis. Main street, lower gymnasium and Byzantine fortifications

Right Marble statue of Hermes 'Propylaios' (before the gates) from Pergamum. Second century. Roman copy of a work by Alkamenes. Istanbul Archaeological Museums. The inscription reads: 'You will recognise the fine statue by Alkamenes, the Hermes before the Gates. Pergamios gave it. Know thyself.' Alkamenes is known to have been active *c* 440–400 BC and to be from Athens.

construction and maintenance of roads, cisterns, pools and houses in Pergamum. The one known as the 'police inscription' is displayed in Bergama Museum. The magnificent head of Alexander the Great which is on display in Istanbul Archaeological Museums was found in the earth during excavations carried out in this area. It is thought to have have fallen down from one of the houses that stood on the higher ground.

Excavations have also shown that the area to the west of the agora was also occupied by houses.

GATE OF EUMENES

During the reign of Eumenes II, the upper, middle and lower acropolis were all surrounded by walls. Access to the city was a big entryway with three towers, situated to the south of the lower agora. This entrance had a large courtyard and owing to the curve of the main street at this point the visitor had to go through two gates. In other words, in order to reach the main street a visitor, after having entered by one gate, took a few steps to the left and making another turn in the same direction emerged from a second gate. To make this rather unusual way of entry attractive, a portico was built on the other side of the courtyard.

The main street of antiquity began at this gate, turned sharply to the east and went up by the house of consul Attalos, the shops, gate of middle gymnasium, and the public fountain like a long snake and, making another sharp turn in the opposite direction, climbed up by the terrace above the sanctuary of Hera, past the living quarters, and the baths, and crossing the upper agora reached the citadel gate.

Marble head of Alexander the Great. First half of second century BC. Istanbul Archaeological Museums. The head comes from the excavations carried out at the lower agora of Pergamum, and is thought to have fallen down from the houses occupying the area above the market. Some archaeologists believe that it belonged to one of the statues of the altar of Zeus. The great mane rising from the middle of the forehead and falling to the sides in uneven locks is characteristic of Alexander. It is thought to have been inspired by the portrait head of the hero sculpted by Lysippos in the fourth century BC. The pathos and softness of expression are typic of the Pergamane school of sculpture.

Lower agora. The doors and back wall of shops

TEMPLE OF SERAPIS
(RED HALL)

The most conspicuous building in ancient Pergamum – and also today's Bergama – was the temple dedicated to the Egyptian gods. Owing to the colour of its red brickwork, which in some places still retains its original marble facing, it is popularly known as the 'Red Hall'.

The temple consisted of a main building and two lateral buildings. All of these were preceded by a large forecourt measuring some 200 x 100 meters. The forecourt was flanked by porticoes. The central four columns of the east portico constituted a kind of monumental entrance. Access to the main building was by a huge door approximately 7 meters wide and 14 meters high. The monolithic marble threshold measures some 7.5 x 2 metres and weighs about 35 tons. Two holes 5 meters apart, on the marble indicate that the entrance probably had a bronze door of two pieces. The floor and the walls of the edifice were faced with marble. A balcony resting on columns encircled the interior of which the first half was lit by windows (probably with glass) placed above the recesses – five on each side. The area where the actual ceremonies took place was left in semidarkness. At the very end of the side porticoes two stairways led to the balcony and the roof.

The centre of the floor was occupied by a shallow depression and a deep drain, both full of water. This was followed by a high podium (1.5 m) on which a large base (4.6 x 4.6 m) with the cult statue, probably 10 meters high, stood. The passage which goes through the podium and comes up through a hole in the middle of the base probably enabled the priests to 'make the god speak'.

During the Byzantine era, the main building was turned into a church, whose walls are still partly surviving, dedicated to St John the Apostle. Some

Temple of Serapis

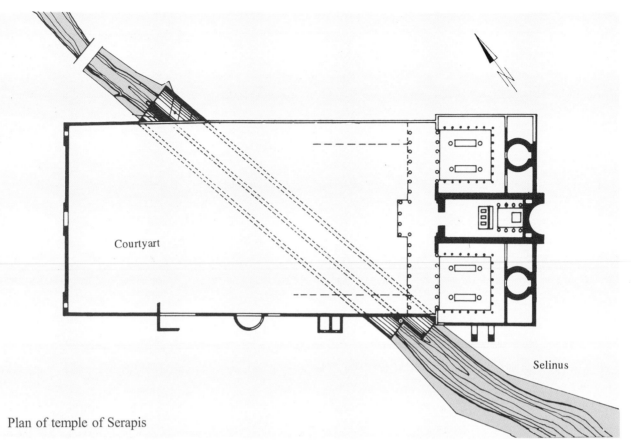

Courtyard

Selinus

Plan of temple of Serapis

Temple of Serapis

material from the temple was obviously reused in the construction of the church.

The structures which flank the main building have tower-like circular architecture made of unworked stone and lime mortar and covered with small hewn stones. Their courtyards also contained long pools with circular smaller pools at each end, and were surrounded with stoas on three sides. The roofs of these stoas were supported by twice life-size statues which were carved as a male figure (atalant) on one side and a female figure (caryatid) on the other side. Some featured female figures on both sides. The heads, arms and feet of these statues were sculpted separately and from black marble. According to Greek mythology Atlas supports the vault of heaven at the ends of the earth, and hence 'atlante' is used for the male supporter. Caryatid, according to Vitruvius (active about 25 BC), derives from the ladies in Caryae in Peloponnessus, who danced with a high, round basket-like hat on their heads.

The statues, the pools which symbolized the river Nile and the fact that the building is oriented in a western direction, make one think that the temple must have been dedicated to Serapis, and to the associated goddess Isis and the god Harpocrates. It is known that the Egyptian gods and religious practices became a fashion in the second century in the Roman world. This edifice was erected during the reign of Hadrian (117–138).

The river Selinus still runs diagonally below the big courtyard of the temple in two vaulted canals of 196 meters each, as it used to do during the time that the temple was in use.

Temple of Serapis. Caryatid

Temple of Serapis

SANCTUARY OF ASCLEPIOS (ASCLEPION)

According to Pausanias the cult of Asclepios was first introduced to Pergamum from Epidauros by Archias who was cured there from a 'sprain he got hunting on Pindasos.' Excavations have shown that the history of the Asclepion of Pergamum dates back to the fourth century BC when it must have been founded from the parent temple at Epidauros. The modest cult centre must have developed during the Hellenistic age and reached its peak during the Roman period. Throughout the history of Pergamum while the acropolis protected itself easily during the sieges and raids, the Asclepion, being situated on low ground, was easily captured and sacked and thus suffered more. In the fourth century, parallel to the growth of Christianity, the cult lost its popularity. The site was gradually covered with the silt of spring torrents, which protected its marble from ending up in lime kilns, and thus reached the time that the excavations began in better condition than the acropolis.

A large part of the surviving ruins of the Asclepion at Pergamum date from the first half of the second century, the reign of Hadrian (117–138), the rest being built Antoninus Pius (138–161). The present ruins begin with a magnificent colonnade which was the Sacred Way. This road of about one kilometer began as a vaulted street (via tecta) with a high arched gate – 'Viran kapı' or 'Ruined Gate' – which belonged to the Roman theatre. The colonnaded section was paved with large and even hewn blocks and flanked with porticos along its entire length. About 150 meters before it reached the sanctuary, the via tecta

Asclepion. Sacred Way

Marble bearded head from Pergamum. First half of the second century BC. Istanbul Archaeological Museums. The head, which comes from the excavations carried out at the monumental fountain on the Sacred Way leading to the sanctuary of Asclepios, brings to mind – owing to the shape of its ears – the head of Marsyas or a satyr. It is twisted violently to one side and features distangled hair and beard. Drill holes in the hair indicate the placement of a metal diadem. At the back it is hollowed out to be fixed ar some background or pole.

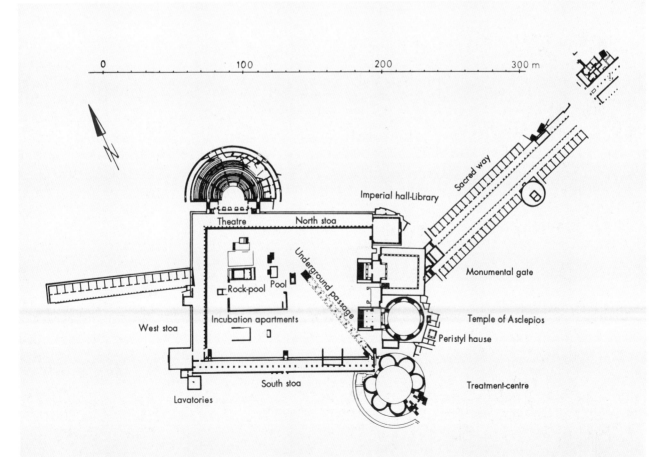

Plan of Asclepion

Asclepion. Piece from the pediment of monumental gate bearing the name of Claudias Charax

was joined by streets coming from other directions. In the past, each visitor, whether coming to the sanctuary to seek a remedy, to avert illness, or to give thanks for continued good health, approached it by the Sacred Way. At the beginning of the surviving section of this colonnade and on the right – northern – side, the remains of a fountain which was built at a later date than the road, catch the eye. Excavations in this section have revealed beautiful statues and reliefs from the Hellenistic and Roman periods. A little further on and on the opposite side are the remains of a round building – thought to be a sepulchral monument probably dating back to the reign of Augustus (31 BC–14 AD).

The Sacred Way ends with a courtyard which is surrounded by stoas on three sides, and access to the sanctuary was by a monumental gate decorated with four Corinthian columns on both sides. The pediment which once stood on top of the columns – and which at present lies on the ground – bears an inscription referring to the Pergamene historian and consul Claudias Charax who commissioned the construction of the gate probably in 142. The monumental gate was particularly important because it separated the profane from the sacred. No death or birth would take place within the sacred area. This practice, which is thought to apply the other sanctuaries of Asclepios as well, had a practical purpose. As the physicians of the present day hesitate to treat patients close to death, in the past it was thought that it would not suit the image of a healer-god if his sanctuary echoed with the wailing of the dying or giving birth, and those who were too sick or expecting were not accepted into the sanctuary.

The square building next to the gate was reserved for the cult of the Emperor. The naked statue of Hadrian during whose reign the reconstruction was began, and which once occupied the central niche of the building, is at present the main attraction of Bergama Museum. The recesses on the walls were for holding the shelves on which the boxes of manuscripts were kept, and show that the room was used as library as well.

To the north, south and west the large earth courtyard was surrounded with stoas. Here, patients or pilgrims, protected from the heat in summer or rain in winter could walk, sit and rest, or discuss their health among themselves, or with the priests. Of these the north stoa has survived to the present in good condition. It was built in the Ionic order. During the disastrous earthquake of 178, the ten columns to the side of the library collapsed. The replacements, which were of Composite order, were shorter, and thus had to be raised on pedestals. While the large rear wall of this colonnade was decorated with marble facing, in order to enable the patients to walk barefoot during certain rites, its floor was of earth, as it was the case with the floor of the large courtyard of the sanctuary.

The maintenance of the sanctuary belonged to a group of priests, wardens and other employees such as door-keepers, bath attendants or singers of the ritual hymns. All of these personnel worked under the authority of a high priest. The priesthood was a prestigious profession, a hereditary lifelong office open only to those from the 'Asclepiad families' of the elite Pergamene society. It is also suggested that the Asclepiads were probably a clan of hereditary physicians, who claimed to be descended from Asclepios.

The sacred theatre of the sanctuary, which was mostly used for the musical or dramatic events, or poetic contests in praise of Asclepios when his festivals were held, could sit about 3,500 people. The area reserved for spectators was semicircular as was the case with Roman theatres. Above the highest row a low gallery, again in accordance with Roman custom, was built. The stage was three-tiered.

The architecture of the stoa to the west of the courtyard was similar to the other one. The columned street which reached the sanctuary on this side opened into the stoa with a doorway. The function of the building next to the doorway is not known. At the end of the stoa and in the corner there was a large room which was probably used for conferences or meetings. Next to this were the lavatories. The men's quarters was a luxurious room which could seat 40 people. Its

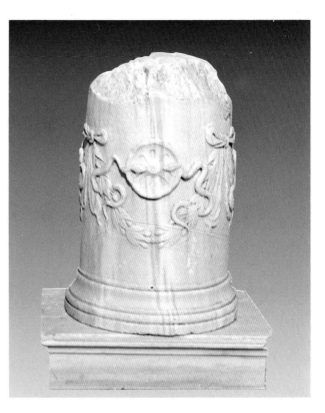

Asclepion. Altar

Asclepion. Forecourt

Above Piece with figure of Nike from the upper gymnasium. Mid–second century. Bergama Museum

Below Piece with figure of Nike from the sanctuary of Asclepion. Mid–second century. Bergama Museum

floor was paved with marble. Some tour guides claim that the base situated at the centre of the floor is thought to have supported the statue of the god Donacacato as it was the case in some Roman toilets. The god was related to the stomach, bowels and digestive system in general. Four Corinthian capitals supported its ceiling, which had a central opening for ventilation and illumination. These capitals are the finest encountered in the sanctuary. The women's quarters was smaller – with only 17 seats – and simpler.

There is almost nothing left from the stoa to the south. The surviving ruins show that it was built over a supporting basement floor.

The remains of three water sources have been located by archaeologists. One of these pools is situated opposite the theatre. Here patients could sit on the low steps inside the pool and take a bath. Chemical analysis has shown that the water of this pool includes radioactive properties. The rocky square south of this pool is thought to be the place where a cult room reserved for Telesphoros, the god of convalescence, and the temples dedicated to Asclepios Soter and the goddess Hygeia stood.

The dry pool which is seen near the entrance of the tunnel was a second source of drinking water. Here water flowed into the fountain through a spout

Right Asclepion. North stoa

Below Marble statue of Hadrian discovered in the Asclepion. Second century. Bergama Museum. The pedestal bears an inscription informing us that the donor of the statue of the 'god' Hadrian was Melitine.

fashioned in the shape of a lion's head and was taken from it in buckets. The remains in andesite and stone workmanship show that during the Hellenistic period a room was built over the pool.

The third pool, referred to by the archaeologists as the 'rock-pool' is situated towards the middle of the west stoa. The marks in the rock on the sides of the pool have led archaeologists to conclude that it had once a roof to keep its water clean, like the other fountains. After the heavy winter and spring rains this area effectually turns into a pool of mud, and it is thought that this pool must have been used for mud-baths. A regular client of the sanctuary, Aristides, mentions that one night at Asclepios' command he woke up, and in bitter cold, 'smeared himself with mud and ran three times round the temples'.

These fountain houses or water basins were used both for medical and religious cleansing purposes, which were inseparable in Greek medicine.

The so-called 'incubation-apartments' or the 'sleeping-apartments' were situated in the southern part of the courtyard and surrounded by walls. The patients would be cured according to the sacred temple sleep, dream or vision. While some patients would be healed directly, in some cases the vision had to be deciphered by the priests, and appropriate medicines prescribed – probably even if the visions

Left Asclepion. Sacred spring
Centre Asclepion. Pool
Below Asclepion. Rock-pool for mud baths

were meaningless. It looks as if in addition to the treatment, the morale they gained by being chosen by Asclepios as being worth of a dream-vision, triggered an improvement in the physical health of the patient. Before leaving the temple, patients gave offerings of thanks, sacrifial animals, cakes, money, or models of the previously afflicted member of the body, a leg, an arm or an ear, to Asclepios. The general impression gained about this treatment is that it began with a brief diagnosis, included a sort of divine manifestation and ended with a cure.

An 80 meters long underground passage (cryptoportico), built in the Roman period, provided the patients with easy access to the treatment-centre in bad weather. It was probably used to protect the patients from the heat of summer as well. The openings in its ceiling helped both ventilation and lightning. Travellers who visit the sanctuary in summer can easily understand what a big relief it was to shelter in this tunnel for a few minutes.

The exact function of the building which is often referred as the 'treatment-centre' has not yet been determined. It is a singular structure of two storeys. It lies on lower ground than the rest of the sanctuary, and is thought to have been erected in the second half of the second century. The main and upper floor had two entrances; one being towards the south stoa, and

Right Asclepion. Hellenistic stoa in the west of the sanctuary

Centre Asclepion. So-called 'incubation' or 'sleeping' apartments

Below Asclepion. Toilets and the substructure of south stoa

the other directly opposite on the southeast side. Its interior is circular and divided into six large apses. The ground floor features stone basins for drinking water which were served by an intricate supply system. Even if the exact function of this rotunda is not known, some kind of medical bathing must have taken place here.

The most beautiful edifice in the sanctuary was the temple of Asclepios. According to Aristides this cylindrical edifice was erected at the expense of L Cuspius Pactumeius Rufinus, who was consul in Rome in the year 142. Its circular form with a dome symbolized the cosmic rule of Zeus-Asclepios-Soter. In plan, though half of its size, the building was a duplicate of the Pantheon in Rome, which was erected during the reign of Hadrian (*c* 125). It began with a monumental gate. In the circular interior seven angular niches alternating with rounded ones created a feeling of movement. The niche opposite the entrance was occupied by a cult statue of Asclepios. In the remaining niches probably the statues of gods and deities associated with health stood. It was lit through an opening at the centre of its dome. Two inseparable names associated with ancient Greek medical treatment are Aristides and Galen, and both were closely related with Pergamum, one being a patient and the other a doctor.

Asclepion. So-called 'treatment centre'

AELIUS ARISTIDES

Although it does not give much information about the existing buildings of the Asclepion of Pergamum, the most intriguing descriptions of temple medicine comes from the records, or *Hieroi Logoi* (*Sacred Discourses*) of the rhetor Aelius Aristides (118–181) who stayed at this sanctuary for a long period.

Aristides was born in 118 in Mysia and enjoyed a good health until his late twenties. He was from a wealthy family and received his education from the most respected teachers of his time. After travelling to the most important cultural centres of the period he began his career in Rome, where he later became sick and was compelled to return home.

In the summer of 145 he received a dream in which he was asked by Asclepios to visit the Asclepion of Pergamum. During his two-year stay in the sanctuary he was treated according to the advice or the interpretation of the advice of the healer-god or the dreams and visions that he had sent to the patient. Sometimes these dreams led to such bizarre prescriptions that the doctors were afraid that the fragile physique of Aristides could not bear them. Also, one of the first orders of Asclepios was that Aristides should make a record of his visions and their cures, so that the rest of the world would benefit from them.

Galen, who may or may not have met Aristides personally, diagnosed him as a consumptive: *I have seen many people whose body was naturally strong and whose soul was weak, inert and useless. Thus their sicknesses have arisen from a sort of insomnia and apoplexy and inervation and sicknesses of the sort of epilepsy... And as to them, whose souls are naturally strong and whose bodies are weak, I have only seen a few of them. One of them was Aristides, one of the inhabitants of Mysia. And this man belonged to the most prominent rank of orators.*

Asclepion . Temple of Asclepius

Although his health did not improve much after all that treatment, Aristides is known to have reached the advanced age of 63.

GALENOS

Galen (*c* 129–199), as he is commonly known in English, is the most famous physician of antiquity after Hippocrates (460– *c* 380 BC) who is known as the first doctor who sought to develop medicine as a science. He was born in Pergamum, and belonged to a family from the upper class Pergamene society. His father is known as Nicon of Pergamum, an architect. After finishing his elementary education, at the age of 16 he began to study medicine. His medical studies took 12 years – an unheard of length of time for the Roman period – and took him to Smyrna, Corinth and Alexandria. At the age of 28 he returned to his native city and was appointed surgeon to a school of gladiators by the high priest of Asclepion, probably in the amphitheatre, where he gained valuable experience working some four or five years. In 162, he travelled to Rome, as a well-known philosopher-physician and after some years became the court physician of the co-emperors Marcus Aurelius and Lucius Verus. His most important works are from this period during which he found time both to study and write.

Galen's prescription is based on three major elements: diet, hot and cold baths, and exercise. Galen's opinions are based on confidence in the human organism to restore itself (a principle he derives from Hippocrates), but especially on direct experimental observation of the ways in which the organs of the human body function.

CULT OF ASCLEPIOS

The generally accepted version of stories about the birth of Asclepios claims that his mother was Coronis, the daughter of a Thessalian king and his father Apollo, the healer-god of the Greek Pantheon. While she is still carrying the child of Apollo, Coronis takes a mortal lover and is punished. In fact Apollo leaves a crow to guard the girl. However, instead of protecting her from the youth the crow flies to Delphi to report her infidelity to the god. The latter becomes angry and turns its feathers black, and all its descendants have been black ever since. While she is on the funeral pyre, Apollo tears out his unborn child and gives him to the care of the Magnesian Centaur Chiron who brings him up. The child learns the art of medicine from the Centaur and when he grows up, becomes a famous doctor. Gradually his healing powers reach such a degree that in addition to making people live very long lives, he begins raising the dead and thus incurs the wrath of Hades the god of the Underworld. Upon the complaint of his brother, Zeus kills Asclepios with a thunderbolt. However, he later relents, and, bringing Asclepios back to life makes him a god.

At the beginning Asclepios was regarded only as a healing spirit. However in the course of time he became popular as the agent of divine cure and by the end of the sixth century BC his cult and priests penetrated into the most distant corners of the Greek world, at sacred springs. The most famous sanctuaries of Asclepios were those at Epidauros, Cos and Pergamum. Many Greek doctors were priests of the cult of Asclepios. When people were ill, they visited

Asclepion. Peristyl house

Marble statue of Marsyas. Roman copy after a Pergamene original of the third century BC. Louvre (Borghese Collection). The hero is shown in his common posture suspended from a tree.

Overleaf Marble relief depicting the building of Auge's ark. Frieze from the wall surrounding the altar of offerings of the altar of Zeus. Mid–second century BC. Pergamum Museum, Berlin

one of the temples of the healer-god. There the physician-priests offered both ordinary medicines and the hope of a miraculous cure. After having arrived at the sanctuary, sick people first had to perform sacrifices and purification ceremonies. Then they slept in the special rooms expecting that Asclepius would heal them while they slept. Sometimes he appeared in a dream and revealed what treatment would cure them. In case he could not appear personally, he would send dream visions which the priests would decipher and prescribe accordingly during the following day. Parallel to his popularity, myths about Asclepios multiplied. In the *Iliad* his sons Machaon and Podaleirios are doctors in the Greek lines. Of his wife Epione and five daughters, only one of his daughters, Hygeia, rose to prominence, and became the personification of health.

The cult of Asclepios survived until the later Roman period. However, in course of time he lost his status as a healer-god in the physical sense of the word and came to be concerned with spiritual needs, aspirations, anxieties and similar matters.

In art Asclepios is usually shown as a strong middle aged man, with bare or sandalled feet, a cloak slung over his left shoulder. A snake-entwined staff is his most prominent feature. The staff is thought to signify a walking stick used by travelers, and Asclepios as a mortal physician journeyed long distances. It was also a support or relief for the sick. In the pagan world snakes were associated with fertility and healing deities. Since they renew their skin every year and also disappear into the holes at the beginning of winter and reappear in spring, they were taken as the symbol of eternal rebirth. At the sanctuaries of Asclepios snakes harmless to humans were kept.

HISTORY OF PERGAMUM
THE FOUNDATION STORY

When Aleus, King of Tegea in Arcadia, is on a visit to Delphi, the Oracle of Apollo warns him that harm will come to his family from the descendants of his daughter. Aleus hurries home and in order to prevent his daughter, Auge, from becoming a mother, appoints her a priestess of Athena. However, this does not protect the young girl, and Heracles during his visit to Tegea violates the virgin-priestess. When Auge gives birth to Telephus, Aleus orders an ark to be built, and shutting his daughter in it, casts the vessel out to sea. The waves take the ark to the mouth of the river Caicus(Bakır çay) in Asia Minor, where King Teuthros of Mysia meets and welcomes her. He adopts – in some versions of the myth marries – Auge. Telephus is left behind by his mother in the wilderness. Here, Heracles finds his son.

Having grown to manhood Telephus travels to Arcadia, and as prophesied kills the sons of King Aelus. Afterwards he goes to Asia Minor and becomes King of Mysia. In one of his adventures he leads the Greeks to Troia and after the victory, on his return, lays the foundation of the city of Pergamum. This story is probably based on the recollection of the emigrations from Greece to Mysia and the rest of the coast of western Anatolia during and towards the end of the Dark Ages of Anatolia (*c* 1100–800 BC). Nevertheless, through Telephus, the Attalids were to claim their descent from Heracles, and thus from Zeus.

The pottery sherds brought to light during excavations show that the history of the first settlement on the acropolis goes back to the 8th century BC, the Archaic period, probably by non-Hellenic people.

The acropolis of Pergamum is a formidable rocky mountain – some 330 meters – rising sharply from the plain, and accessible only from the south. Strabo has described it as 'a mountain in the form of a pineapple'. It is encircled by the tributaries of the river Caicus, Cetius (Kestel çayı) on the east, and Selinus (Bergama çayı) on the west.

The first historical reference to Pergamum is encountered in the work of Xenophon, *Anabasis*. In about 399 BC Greek mercenaries passed through the town on their way back from Persia. (Greek mercenaries wanted to support the revolt of Cyrus the Younger against his brother Artaxerxes II (Mnemon) (404–359 BC) of Persia. However, in the battle of Cunaxa Cyrus the Younger was to be killed, and the Greek soldiers were to decide to return home. *Anabasis* is the story of this long march by way of Trapezus, Thrace and Byzantium). During this period the city seems to have been ruled by a certain Gongylus, and to have a population of local people, nominally Persian subjects.

The Persian rule over in western Anatolia came to an end with the defeat of the Persian army by Alexander the Great at Granicus in 334 BC. Following this battle, the cities of western Anatolia including Pergamum gained their independence.

Marble relief depicting Heracles and his son Telephus, being suckled by a lioness. Frieze from the wall surrounding the altar of offerings of the altar of Zeus. Mid-second century BC. Pergamum Museum, Berlin

THE ATTALIDS

The history of the city which is the subject of this thin volume begins with one Philetairos, lasted for a brief period of 150 years, and ended with Attalos III. During this brief history Pergamum was ruled by kings of Attalid blood.

Philetairos (281–263 BC)

After the unexpected death of Alexander the Great in 323 BC, in Babylon, his generals shared out his large empire. Antigonus I the One-eyed took Macedonia, Seleucus I Nicator Syria and Ptolemy I Soter Egypt. Western Anatolia, with its valuable natural resources and geographical position on the major trade routes, became an area of conflict between the Antigonid and Seleucid Kingdom. It seems that the birth of Pergamum as an independent kingdom owes much to its geographical location between these two rival Hellenistic powers and also to its clever rulers who were able to use this situation for their advantage. In buying up allies, buying off enemies or playing on rivalries they were relentless.

Antiochus I of the Seleucid Kingdom, assisted by Lysimachus – one of the former generals of Alexander – defeated the Antigonid army at the battle of Ipsus in Phrygia, in 301 BC. In the sharing of spoils, Thrace and Anatolia as far as the Taurus fell to the share of Lysimachus. Lysimachus appointed a local governor, a half – Macedonian and half – Paphlagonian eunuch (said to have been injured in infancy and a mercenary officer in the army of Antigonus I) Philateiros to Pergamum and granted him a large part of his treasury, a sum of nine thousand talents. When Lysimachus (during whose reign Hellenistic Ephesus was also built), was defeated by Antiochus I of Seleucid Kingdom and lost his life in 281 BC at the battle of Corupedion near Magnesia, Philateiros found himself in control of Pergamum and owner of a large treasury. Philateiros was a good administrator and during his 22 year rule he used this money to keep his position. Assuring the Seleucids of his loyalty to them he established his own kingdom, began to beautify his city by building temples and other public buildings, created a strong army and established good relations with his neighbours.

Eumenes I (263–241 BC)

When Philetairos died, he was succeeded by Eumenes I, his nephew and adopted son. Eumenes made an alliance with Egypt and during the second year of his reign, in 262 BC, the new king defeated Antiochus I of the Seleucid Kingdom in a battle near Sardis, thus confirming his independence, and began to extend the frontiers of his small kingdom. Though he did not assume the title, Eumenes is regarded as the first 'king' of Pergamum. He continued the policy of his uncle to strengthen his kingdom politically and economically. During his reign the coastal town of Elea near the mouth of Caicus river was developed into a port.

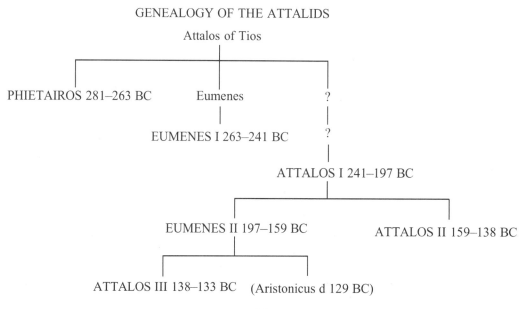

GENEALOGY OF THE ATTALIDS

Attalos of Tios

PHIETAIROS 281–263 BC   Eumenes   ?

EUMENES I 263–241 BC   ?

ATTALOS I 241–197 BC

EUMENES II 197–159 BC   ATTALOS II 159–138 BC

ATTALOS III 138–133 BC   (Aristonicus d 129 BC)

Attalos I (241–197 BC)

At his death, he was succeeded by Attalos I – a kinsman, and probably the only surviving male in the lineage at that time, his adopted son.

Attalos I was a shrewd politician who ruled for 44 years. During his reign he exploited the chaotic conditions of his time; keeping up his struggle with the Seleucid kings and establishing good relations with Rome and fortfeiting its confidence. In his struggle with the Gauls, he refused to pay tribute to them, as the Pergamene kings before him had done, and decided to fight. His soldiers were terrified of facing these formidable warriors; it is said that when the sacrifice was made before the battle the words 'victory for the king' appeared on the liver of the sacrifice. In this manner, the king's soldiers took heart and defeated the Gauls. After the war, it became clear that Attalos I had written the words backwards on his hand and while inspecting the entrails of the victim, had imprinted the words on its liver.

Eumenes II (197–159 BC)

His eldest son and successor Eumenes II was an able and energetic ruler. During his reign the Roman army under Lucius Cornelius Scipio (brother of Scipio Africanus) entered Asia Minor and after joining forces with him, defeated Antiochus III at the battle of Magnesia in 190 BC. The hero of the battle was Eumenes II who faced and broke the armoured Persian horsemen in the enemy ranks. After the battle Rome allowed Pergamum to take over most of the Seleucid possessions in Asia Minor, asking all cities that formerly paid tribute to Pergamum to continue paying the same sum; and all cities which formerly paid tribute to the Seleucids were to pay the same amount to Pergamum

Eumenes II did everything to make his city a typical Hellenistic capital. The famous library, the fortifications, the altar of Zeus and most of the temples and public buildings were built during his reign. This material and cultural progress of Pergamum continued during the rule of his brother and successor Attalos II as well. In addition to the edifices built in Pergamum Attalos II is remembered with the stoa he commissioned in Athens. Attalos II was known to have sent money to Delphi and Eumenes II grain to Rhodes to meet the payment of teachers of

Statuette of a bearded man fighting, thought to be from Pergamum. Mid–second century BC. Bronze incrusted in silver and red copper. Louvre

children. There is no reason not to think that the same was done in Pergamum. Also, it is known that at least some girls received a degree of education in Pergamum, a practice which was not in the traditional Greek education system.

The economic, political and administrative system that the Attalids established in Pergamum was, in its general outline, similar to the other–rival–Hellenistic capitals such as Antioch-on-the-Orontes (today's Antakya) of the Seleucid Kingdom, or Alexandria, the capital of Ptolemaic Egypt: an absolute monarchy working through a centralized bureaucracy. The natural resources of the kingdom, the gold and silver and lead mines and the imperial work shops belonged to the rulers. The workers in the king's workshops which produced woven and dyed fabrics, pottery and metalwork were mostly the native Lydians. The agricultural products of the area included wine, oil, grain, stockbreeding (horses, hogs, sheep and thus a flourishing textile industry), and pitch and timber for ship-building. The king also owned the land which was tilled by dependent farmers (serfs). He also had the right to attach land or villages to temples or bestow them on dignitaries, who were mostly members of the Macedonian nobility. Tax revenues from the conquered provinces also constituted an important portion of the financial resources of the kingdom.

During the rule of the Attalids the acropolis of Pergamum was transformed into one of the finest Hellenistic citadels of the time. While its self-sufficient economy attracted common unemployed crowds from Greece the challenging building programs of its rulers attracted some of the best sculptors and architects of the period. Here, under the rule of the cultivated Attalid kings, these artists turned the city into a copy of Athens; a new centre of Greek art, literature and science, which found its best expression in architecture and fine arts. A small copy of Athena Parthenos, the famous gold and ivory cult image created by Phidias for the temple on the acropolis of Athens, stood in the library of Pergamum.

Among the many scholars who were attracted by the Attalid patrons of art and culture was Apollonius of Perge, one of the greatest mathematicians of the time, who is said to have studied for a while in Pergamum as a guest of Attalos I, and dedicated some of his books to him. Apollonius is known to have sought to explain the apparent movements of the stars, or 'heavenly bodies', by a combination of epicycles and eccentric circles. Also his work *On Conics* is regarded as one of the masterpieces of Greek mathematics. The terms by which the three

Roman city. Amphitheatre

types of conic sections are known, 'ellipse', 'parabola', and 'hyperbola' derive from him. Stoic grammarian Crates of Mallos was one of the most famous scholars working in Pergamum at the time of Eumenes II. Apollodoros of Athens also is known to have dedicated his verse *Chronicle* to Attalos II.

Attalos II (160–138 BC)

The policy of Pergamum did not change during the reign of the son and successor of Eumenes II. The new king was very popular with Rome. Nevertheless, even if he established Attalia (today's Antalya) as a port of entry into Pamphylia, he showed every effort not to offend Rome, which had set its greedy eyes on the wealth of Asia Minor a long time ago.

Attalos III (138–133 BC)

Attalos II was succeeded by a weak and eccentric nephew, Attalos III. He was interested in zoology, husbandry and metalworking and neglected the affairs of state. His shortcomings gave Rome a chance to increase its influence in the affairs of Pergamum. Meanwhile Rome had become so powerful that, there seemed little chance for an independent kingdom in Asia Minor and thus Attalos III's decision to turn over his kingdom to Rome has a certain logic about it. When he died, it was discovered that he had bequeathed his private fortune, royal lands and subject cities to Rome. However, four years had to pass until Rome established its wealthy new province of Asia. Aristonicus who claimed to be a son of Eumenes II by a concubine, claimed his right to the kingdom and led a popular and nationalistic revolt supported by the peasants and native tribesmen against the empire. In 129 BC he was defeated and put to death and Pergamum was incorporated in the future Roman Empire.

ROMAN CITY

Rome respected Pergamum and regarded it as a free city. Though not comparable to the Attalid period, during Roman rule Pergamum remained a rich and cultured city. In 88 BC, together with Ephesus and other cities in the region, Pergamum also joined forces with Mithridates VI (120–63 BC), King of Pontus, and participated in the massacre of ten thousands of the Roman colonists living in western Asia Minor. When the Roman general Sulla drove Mithridates out of Asia, Pergamum had lost its freedom and become a Roman city. From then on, the fortunes of the city were parallel to those of the empire, and together they began to decline in the third century. Much of the construction dating from this period has been carried out using the older and already existing building materials. During this late Roman period some sturdy Hellenistic constructions, such as the terrace of the sanctuary of Demeter and the upper gymnasium were incorporated as bulwarks in the fortifications.

Research and the surviving ruins have shown that the area lying between the river Selinus and the Asclepion was settled during the Roman era. During this period the total population of Pergamum is thought to have been around 150,000 people. The sacred road by which one reached the Asclepion began in the Roman city. It is known that a stadium, a theatre and an amphitheatre were built in this area. The last was built on two sides of a side-branch of the river Selinus, which was vaulted over, and during the staging of mock sea-battles, its water could be channeled into the performance area. In that area settled during the Roman period no excavation has been yet made.

The tumulus of 'Mal Tepe' (Treasure Hill) situated among the modern apartments of Bergama, is thought to be related to the Roman history of the city. According to a version of the foundation legend, Auge married the King of Mysia, Teuthras, and when he died she was buried at Pergamum. Pausanius relates that 'Auge's monument is at Pergamos on the Kaikos, a tumulus on earth surrounded by a stone platform and surmounted by a naked woman in bronze.' Although research has shown that the origin of the Mal tepe tumulus does not go further back than the Roman period, it is a tempting idea that this tumulus, which is surmounted with the remains of a monument (a statue base?), and contains the remains of a tomb chamber was originally the tomb of Auge. A second tumulus known as 'Yığma Tepe' probably belonged to of the Hellenistic kings. The tomb chamber, which must have existed, has not yet been located.

Roman city. 'Viran Kapı' or the 'Ruined Gate' leading to the Asclepion and theatre

CHRISTIANITY IN PERGAMUM

It is thought that by the second half of the 1st century a local congregation of Christians existed in Pergamum.

The city was one of the Seven Churches of Apocalypse (the other six being Ephesus, Smyrna, Sardes, Philadelphia, Thyatira and Laodicea). St John the Apostle in his Revelation 2:12–17 states:

To the angel of the church in Pergamum write:

' This is the message from the one who has the sharp two-edged sword. I know where you live, there where Satan has his throne. You are true to me, and you did not abandon your faith in me even during the time when Antipas, a faithful witness for me, was killed there where Satan lives. But here are a few things I have against you: there with you are some who follow the teaching of Balaam, who taught Balak how to cause the people of Israel to sin by eating food that had been offered to idols, and by committing immorality. In the same way, you also have people among you who follow the teaching of the Nicolaitans.

Turn from your sins, then! If not, I will come to you soon and fight against those people with the sword that comes out of my mouth.

'If you have ears, then, listen to what the Spirit says to the churches!

'To those who have won the victory I will give some of the hidden manna. I will also give each of them a white stone, on which a new name is written, which no one knows except the one who receives it.

In the first part the letter discusses the problems encountered among the Christians in Pergamum. It seems that despite their faith in the new religion, some of them were practicing the heresy of Balaam. Jewish tradition (Numbers 22–24) identifies Balaam, a magician who cursed the Israelites to prevent them from entering the Jordan Valley, with idolatry and temple prostitution. He convinced the Israelites to 'eat food sacrificed to idols. Eating meat sacrificed to idols was encountered also in Corinth for which St Paul has reproached them in 1 Cor 10:14–22. There are also those who believe the teaching of the Nicolaitans. Nicolas, a proselyte of Antioch, and one of the seven deacons of Jerusalem in the first century, became the originator of an early heresy which was named after him. His purpose was to achieve a compromise between Christianity and the prevailing social norms of the time, by reconciling the observance of certain pagan practices with membership in the Christian community. After having acknowledged the problems in Pergamum, St John admonishes those who waver to repent and threatens them that Christ will come for them. The believers who keep their faith will be rewarded.

It is assumed that in Pergamum as elsewhere the Christian community included some Hellenistic Jewish converts. Although a gable from a synagogue door or screen of the Greco-Roman period showing a menorah has been discovered, the place where the synogogue was located is not known.

While some scholars claimed that when St John referred to the 'seat of Satan' he had the altar of Zeus in mind, others believe that this was an allusion of the mystical chest (cyst) in which was kept a live serpent, a special object of veneration in the Asclepion, or the sanctuary itself. It is also claimed that St John was concerned with the idolatry of emperor worship more than the established Hellenic cults, and thus 'Satan's throne' was probably the cult of the Emperor.

Apostolic Constitutions states that the first bishop of Pergamum was Gaius, whom John the Elder addressed in his third letter: *My dear friend, you are so faithful in the work you do for the brothers . . . They have spoken of your love to the church here . . .* After Gaius, Antipas became the spiritual leader of Pergamene congregation. He was believed to have been a dentist and died a martyr, being roasted in a brazen bull (St Polycarp and St Eustace were also believed to suffer similar ends).

Christian literature of early martyrdom gives the impression that Pergamum received its share of the persecutions caused by the edict of the Roman Emperor Decius (249–251) which ordered all the people in his empire to 'sacrifice to the gods'.

Pergamum was the second stop of the Roman governor Quintilianus in the spring of 250. After having already sentenced Pionius to crucifixion in Ephesus, in mid-April he arrived at Pergamum. Here refusing to 'sacrifice to the gods', three Christians, Carpus, the bishop of Thyatira, Papylus, the deacon of Thyatira, and a woman named Agathonice were sentenced to be burned alive in the amphitheatre. Fearing that the April rains would start soon, the order was carried out immediately. As the crowd hurried to bring the fire Papylus is said to have addressed them thus: *Here the fire burns briefly, but there it burns for ever, and by it, God will judge the world. It will drown the sea, the mountains and the woods. By it, God will judge each human soul.* When Agathonice was urged not to make her children motherless by her obstinacy, she is known to have replied *God will look after them.*

The church of Pergamum took an active part in the early religious movements until the eighth century at which time the whole area suffered Arab raids. The last Christian church of Haghia Sophia was turned into the Ulu Cami, or Grand Mosque, in 1398.

Archaeological research has revealed the remains of a number churches in ancient Pergamum. The best known of these was the church of St John the Apostle, which was built into the so-called Red Court, and still retains some of its walls. A second church had been built in the courtyard of the lower agora and has no visible remains at present. A third one occupied the site of the temple of Athena and dated to the reign of Justinian the Great (527–565). There are no visible remains of the churches which were built on the theatre terrace and in the living quarters.